GARLAND STUDIES IN

ENTREPRENEURSHIP

edited by
STUART BRUCHEY
ALLAN NEVINS PROFESSOR EMERITUS
COLUMBIA UNIVERSITY

A GARLAND SERIES

ENTREPRENEURIAL OPPORTUNITY RECOGNITION THROUGH SOCIAL NETWORKS

ROBERT P. SINGH

GARLAND PUBLISHING, INC.
A MEMBER OF THE TAYLOR & FRANCIS GROUP
NEW YORK & LONDON / 2000

338.04
S61e

Published in 2000 by
Garland Publishing, Inc.
A member of the Taylor & Francis Group
29 West 35th Street
New York, NY 10001

10 9 8 7 6 5 4 3 2 1

Library of Congress Cataloging-in-Publication Data

Singh, Robert P. (Robert Paul). 1969-
    Entrepreneurial opportunity recognition through social
    networks / Robert P. Singh.
JK   p. cm — (Garland studies in entrepreneurship)
    Includes bibliographical references and index.
    ISBN 0-8153-3813-X (alk. paper)
    1. Entrepreneurship—Psychological aspects. 2.
    Recognition (Psychology) 3. Social networks. 4.
    Business networks. 5. New business enterprises. I. Title.
    II. Series.
    HB615 .S563 2000
    338'.004—dc21

                                              00-021547

Printed on acid-free, 250 year-life paper
Manufactured in the United States of America

To the love of my life, Lisa,
and
our little angel, Jade.

Table of Contents

List of Tables

List of Figures

ENTREPRENEURIAL OPPORTUNITY RECOGNITION THROUGH SOCIAL NETWORKS

CHAPTER 1

Introduction

The number of new businesses founded annually in the United States continues to grow (Kirchoff and McAuliffe, 1989; Kirchoff and Phillips, 1992; Gupta, 1995) and, given the levels of downsizing in large firms (i.e., Cameron, 1994; Seppa, 1996; Serwer, 1995), increasingly affordable information technology that creates significant competitive advantages (Hammer and Champy, 1993; Lawless and Anderson, 1996), and other basic factors, the high rate of new business formations will continue. As a result of the growing number of new entrepreneurial firms in the United States and economies around the world, there is increasing interest in the processes that lead to successful entrepreneurship.

Previous entrepreneurship research and theory development has studied individual differences and personal characteristics of entrepreneurs (e.g., Brenner, 1987; Brockhaus, 1980; Kalleberg and Leicht, 1991; McClelland, 1961); however, the literature has not shown agreement on a unique profile of the entrepreneur. A number of studies have found no support for differences between entrepreneurs and managers or other reference samples (Low and MacMillan, 1988; Sexton and Bowman, 1984; Stuart and Abetti, 1990).

Although researchers have not completely agreed on a definition of "entrepreneur" and "entrepreneurship" (e.g., Carland et al., 1988; Gartner, 1988; Stearns and Hills, 1996; Vesper, 1996), one variable that is unique to the field of entrepreneurship is *opportunity recognition*. Yet, as Hills (1995) points out, unlike opportunity *evaluation*, opportunity recognition has received little attention in the academic literature. How and where entrepreneurs identify the concepts for their businesses remains elusive and continues to go relatively unstudied. This is surprising because without the recognition of the opportunity, entrepreneurship cannot take place.

In the past decade, entrepreneurship researchers have focused on entrepreneurship as a process (e.g., Bull and Willard, 1993; Bygrave and Hofer, 1991; Covin and Slevin, 1991; Gartner, 1988; Lumpkin and Dess, 1996), and opportunity recognition may be the critical first step of the process (Christensen et al., 1994; Hills, 1995; Timmons et al., 1987). Bygrave (1989a, 1989b) calls the founding of an organization to pursue an *entrepreneurial opportunity* the "Entrepreneurial Event." Similarly, Stevenson and Jarillo-Mossi (1986) view entrepreneurship as the process of creating value by combining resources to *exploit an opportunity.* And, the pursuit of the opportunity may occur regardless of resources controlled (Stevenson et al., 1989). Bygrave and Hofer (1991) acknowledge that entrepreneurs come in all shapes and sizes and propose a broad definition of the entrepreneur as "someone who *perceives an opportunity* and creates an organization to pursue it." (p. 14). The above definitions underscore the critical importance of *opportunity* to entrepreneurship.

But what constitutes an opportunity? Definitions of "opportunity" vary (e.g., Kirzner, 1973; McMullan and Long, 1990; Schumpeter, 1934; Stevenson et al., 1989; Timmons, 1994b). An opportunity goes beyond the business idea to include contextual/ environmental factors (Bygrave, 1994; Timmons, 1994a; 1994b). But where an idea ends and an opportunity begins is not clearly delineated. To date, no one has surveyed the literature and provided a thorough definitional discussion of the opportunity construct. This is remarkable considering how important it is to the very essence of entrepreneurship. In Chapter 2, a definitional discussion is provided to clarify the opportunity construct.

Once "opportunity" has been defined, the next question is *how do entrepreneurs recognize opportunities?* Using field studies and survey methods, Christensen and Peterson (1990) concluded that, in addition to profound market or technological knowledge, specific problems and social encounters are often a source of venture ideas. Consistent with this finding, using a sample of 65 randomly selected entrepreneurs, Koller (1988) found that half learned of the opportunity through their social network, while the other half recognized the opportunity individually. Further, he discovered significant differences in the types of opportunities identified between the two groups. More specifically, those who identified ideas for their business individually were more likely to use prior experience and be motivated out of a "desire for entrepreneurship" than those who got their ideas from their social network. Hills et al., (1997) reported that entrepreneurs who used network sources to learn of entrepreneurial opportunities (labeled "network entrepreneurs" in their paper) identified significantly more opportunities than those who developed their venture ideas individually ("solo entrepreneurs").

A social network is defined as "a set of nodes (e.g., persons, organizations) linked by a set of social relationships (e.g., friendship, transfer of funds, overlapping membership) of a specified type" (Laumann et al., 1978: p. 458). Most people have contact, frequent or sporadic, with a great many other people (Boissevain, 1974; Burt, 1986; Pool and Kochen, 1978), and an individual's personal or egocentric social network consists of all of the people (nodes) that the individual knows both well and not so well (Barnes, 1972; Mitchell, 1969). Studies suggest that personal networks of entrepreneurs may be critical to the entrepreneurial process (Dubini and Aldrich, 1991). Johannisson (1990; p. 41) describes entrepreneurs' personal networks as the "most significant resource of the firm." Entrepreneurship arises from the exploitation of disequilibrium created by the unequal access to information by different market participants (Gilad et al., 1989), but no economic actor has perfect information with which to make rational choices and decisions. Individuals are limited in their ability to process and store information which results in bounded rationality (Simon, 1976). An entrepreneur's social network can help expand the boundaries of rationality by allowing access to knowledge from which to assess and determine a course of action. Through social network ties, a good business idea/opportunity may be identified, screened and assessed, and then, if appropriate, acted upon.

Network analysis considers the relational interactions between individuals, groups, and organizations (Burt, 1984; Granovetter, 1985; Powell, 1990), and it captures the emergent processes of organizing (Gartner et al., 1992; Larson and Starr, 1993). From social network theory perspectives, weak ties (Granovetter, 1973) and structural holes and social frontiers (Burt, 1992) within a network may be indicators of accessibility to information that can help a potential entrepreneur recognize an opportunity. Weak ties are casual acquaintances who require little time or energy to maintain the relationships (as opposed to strong ties). A friend of a friend, or a casual business contact would be considered a weak tie. Granovetter (1973) argued that these "low maintenance" individuals are often the source of unique information.

Burt (1992) argues that it is not the strength of the tie that predicts access to information, but rather the number of structural holes within the network. By structural holes, he is referring to non-linkages within a network. For example, a group of four friends, all of whom know each other and spend all of their time together, would have no holes within their network (no non-linkages). However, an individual with three friends, none of whom know each other, would have three holes (non-linkages among all three of the individual's friends). Theoretically, the individual in the second example has access to more information because his/her friends are more likely to have contact with other people (i.e., information sources) outside the immediate network. The density of the network is indicated by the number of structural holes in the network. Burt (1992) also points out the theoretical importance of social frontiers within the network. A social frontier exists between network ties. The more different two network ties are to each other in terms of demographic characteristics (gender, race, religion, etc.), the wider the social frontier and the more likely the exchange of *unique* information. Burt points out that heterogeneity within the network usually increases the number of structural holes, because there is less commonality among network contacts. From the above discussion, it is quite possible that an entrepreneur's social network structure and the quality of ties within the network may be predictors of an individual's opportunity recognition capability.

Kirzner (1973; 1979) suggests that the central role of the entrepreneur is to find and exploit opportunities by taking advantage of economic disequilibria. This is done by recognizing or knowing things that others do not. Kirzner (1979) also points out that entrepreneurs do not have to possess specific knowledge themselves; they may be able to recognize how other people's knowledge, experience, and expertise can be harnessed and employed in a new configuration for profit. Thus, social encounters and network contacts may be important factors in the opportunity recognition process. Studying the differences between opportunities recognized through social networks versus other sources may help to shed light on the enigmatic entrepreneurship process. Over the last decade, entrepreneurial study has expanded to include research on social networks (e.g., Aldrich et al., 1987; Birley, 1985; Dubini and Aldrich, 1991; Hansen, 1995; Tjosvold and Weicker, 1993; Zhao and Aram, 1995). However, aside from the exploratory research conducted by Koller (1988) and Hills et al., (1997), no one has empirically researched the relationship between social networks of entrepreneurs and opportunity recognition. This study seeks to address this research opportunity by studying how and why social network ties are important to the recognition of entrepreneurial opportunities. The broad research objectives are:

1. To explore the opportunity recognition process.
2. To study the literature on the nature of opportunities and to provide a definitional discussion of the entrepreneurial opportunity construct.
3. To present a conceptual/theoretical discussion of the importance of entrepreneurs' social networks to opportunity recognition.
4. To empirically test hypotheses related to opportunity recognition through social networks.
5. To present and discuss new research avenues with respect to opportunity recognition.

The research objectives of this study are met through both conceptual/theoretical development and empirical testing of *a priori* hypotheses. Chapter 2 provides a definitional discussion of "opportunity" and the external forces that create them. In Chapter 3 the current state of the opportunity recognition literature is reviewed and summarized. In Chapter 4, formal hypotheses are developed based on the opportunity recognition literature and social network theories. A discussion of the research methods utilized to test the hypotheses is provided in Chapter 5 and a sample profile is found in Chapter 6. Chapter 7 discusses the empirical results concerning the differences between ideas and opportunities. Chapter 8 reports the results of the empirical tests and Chapter 9 discusses those results. Chapter 10 provides a summary and discussion of supplementary analyses. Concluding remarks, including practical and theoretical implications and future research directions, are presented in Chapter 11.

For the field of entrepreneurship to further develop, it should distinguish itself from other fields and disciplines such as sociology, marketing, organizational behavior, organizational theory, and strategy (Shane, 1997). Entrepreneurship researchers, in setting the boundaries of the field, must study unique variables not studied in other fields. Opportunity recognition is one of those concepts and this study attempts to shed further light on this construct.

Enterpreneural Opportunities: A Definitional Discussion

Master of human destinies am I.
Fame, love, and fortune on my footsteps wait,
Cities and fields I walk; I penetrate
Deserts and seas remote, and, passing by
Hovel, and mart, and palace, soon or late
I knock unbidden, once at every gate!
If sleeping, wake—if feasting, rise before
I turn away. It is the hour of fate,
And they who follow me reach every state
Mortals desire, and conquer every foe
Save death; but those who doubt or hesitate,
Condemned to failure, penury and woe,
Seek me in vain and uselessly implore—
I answer not, and I return no more.

- John James Ingalls
Opportunity

2.1 CHAPTER 2 INTRODUCTION

While definitions of entrepreneurship vary (e.g., Kirzner, 1973; Schumpeter, 1934; Stevenson et al., 1989; Vesper, 1996), the fundamental activity of entrepreneurship is new venture creation (Gartner, 1985; 1990). As such, one major component of any entrepreneurial venture is the *recognition of the opportunity* by the entrepreneur (e.g., Bhave, 1994; Christensen et al., 1994; Hills, 1995; Timmons et al., 1987). Kirzner (1973; 1979) argues that recognizing economic disequilibria and capitalizing on the subsequent opportunities is the central role of the entrepreneur. Bygrave (1989a, 1989b) calls the founding of an organization to pursue an entrepreneurial opportunity the "Entrepreneurial Event." Some have called entrepreneurship the process of creating value by combining resources to exploit an opportunity (Stevenson and Jarillo-Mossi, 1986), in some cases, regardless of resources controlled (Stevenson et al., 1989). There is no question that entrepreneurs come in all shapes and sizes, and recognizing this fact, Bygrave and Hofer (1991) propose a broad definition of the entrepreneur as "someone who perceives an opportunity and creates an organization to pursue it" (p. 14).

Timmons'(1994b) developed a model of the three crucial driving forces of entrepreneurship which included: (1) the founders (entrepreneurs), (2) the recognition of the opportunity, and (3) the resources needed to found the firm. Surrounding the process are such factors as risk, chaos, information asymmetries, resource scarcity, uncertainty, paradoxes, and confusion, all of which complicate the process. Only when all three components *fit* together can successful entrepreneurship take place. The challenge for the entrepreneur is to manipulate and influence the surrounding factors in *real time* to improve the chances for success of the venture. As Timmons (1994b) points out, time does not stand still and the process of recognizing and seizing an opportunity often relies on the right timing.

From the definitions and discussion above, it can be seen that *opportunity is paramount to entrepreneurship*. In fact, Timmons (1994b; p. 30) states that "entrepreneurial achievement is driven by people who search for and shape opportunities." So the question becomes, *What is an entrepreneurial opportunity?* The answer to this fundamental question is critical to understanding entrepreneurship. However, as with the definition of "entrepreneurship," there is confusion in the literature about what constitutes an opportunity. A survey of prior opportunity-related research yields diverse definitions such as a "situation" (Stevenson et al., 1989), economic "disequilibria" (Kirzner, 1973), an "idea leading to a business concept" (Bhave, 1994), or a new "production function" (Schumpeter, 1934). Timmons (1994a; p. 87) argues that an opportunity "has the qualities of being attractive, durable, and timely and is anchored in a product or service which creates or adds value for its buyer or end user." "Opportunity" is very much like "love"—everyone knows what it is, but it is difficult to define because it means different things to different people. It is surprising that entrepreneurship scholars have not attempted to systematically define the opportunity construct and come to a consensus on its meaning, particularly when the opportunity and opportunity recognition constructs are so crucial to the entrepreneurship process. The purpose of this chapter is to summarize the existing relevant literature and provide a conceptual discussion of entrepreneurial opportunities - what they are and where they come from. It concludes with a proposed definition of an entrepreneurial opportunity.

2.2 PRIOR CONCEPTIONS AND DEFINITIONS OF OPPORTUNITY

Webster's Dictionary (1984) defines an opportunity as either " 1. a favorable combination of circumstances" or "2. a chance for advancement." These definitions are obviously broad and leave much room for interpretation with respect to entrepreneurs. A researcher could ask, what are these "circumstances," and what constitutes "advancement?" The innovative entrepreneur who develops a unique product that is widely marketable is different from the one who opens a one-person accounting firm based on years of personal experience. The first entrepreneur may be able to create a new multi-million dollar industry, while the second may make a modest living as a self-employed entrepreneur. In both cases, the individuals may take advantage of opportunities, but in very different ways and with very different profit expectations. Yet, both may be satisfied and consider themselves successful. Based on this discussion, different entrepreneurs may have different definitions of "advancement" and may view different circumstances as being "favorable." It is because of the subjective nature of these terms that we are left to ponder the specific characteristics and elements that lie within the broad dimensions of an opportunity. The first step is to specify the borders of the opportunity construct by reviewing conceptions of opportunity within the entrepreneurship literature.

From an economics discipline viewpoint, an entrepreneurial opportunity is a market imperfection or economic disequilibrium that can be exploited by bringing the market to equilibrium (Kirzner, 1973; 1979). Kirzner states that opportunities (disequilibria) exist because of "the ignorance of the original market participants" (1973; p. 14), and entrepreneurs are those rare individuals who take advantage of these market inefficiencies by knowing or recognizing things that others do not. This implies that opportunities exist all around us in time and space, but it is only those individuals with what Kirzner calls "alertness," who have the ability to recognize them. Figure 1 is used to illustrate Kirzner's view of opportunity.

In Figure 1, a market disequilibrium can be found where the selling price for a good (P_1) is below the equilibrium price (P_e). At P_1, the market would support a rise in price and/or an increase in supply because the demand for the good higher than the current output, Q_1. The entreprenuer in this case would be the individual who recognizes that the good can be sold at a price higher than P_1 (up to P_e), or that Q_2 of the good could be sold at the current price. In either case, there is a new potential for profit. These different between the existing price and quantity sold and the potential price and quantity sold represent opportunities which entrepreneurs can take advantage of.

Entrepreneurial opportunities do not always involve simply achieving a balance between supply and demand. In contrast to Kirzner's view of the entrepreneur as a "market tinkerer" who

Figure 1. Opportunity as market disequilibria.

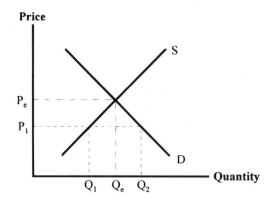

makes adjustments to the market, Schumpeter (1934) views the role of the entrepreneur as a radical market innovator. He discusses the important societal role of the entrepreneur as being the instigator of *creative destruction* through innovation. Schumpeter (1934) argues that industries within societies are replaced by other industries over time. The process of replacement of one industry (destruction) by another more modern industry (creation) is referred to as creative destruction. Tushman and Anderson (1986) illustrate the Schumpeterian model of creative destruction by research findings showing that long periods of incremental changes to markets are broken by technological discontinuities (major technological advances). They argue that, "Major technological innovations represents technical advance so significant that no increase in scale, efficiency, or design can make older technologies competitive with the new technology" (p. 441). Examples include the replacement of the horse-and-buggy by the Model T, or typewriters by computers. With the advent of newer technology, the older technology becomes antiquated and is destroyed.

Schumpeter (1934, p. 66) defines entrepreneurial opportunities as "new production functions where production = 1(choice of products, source of supply, method of productions, method of organization, and choice of markets)." In other words, opportunities emerge when the entrepreneur develops an innovative process and finds a new combination of one or more of the following: (1) new products; (2) new production or organizational methods; (3) new markets; (4) new sources of input; and/or (5) new market structures. Referring to the supply and demand curves illustrated in Figure 1, entrepreneurial opportunities would be innovations to the market which radically transform existing supply and demand curves, or which destroy existing curves and create new supply and demand curves for new products or services which replace outdated similar products or services.

As with Schumpeter, Drucker (1985) stresses the importance of innovation to opportunity. He argues that innovation is "the specific tool of entrepreneurs, the means by which they exploit change as an opportunity for a different business or different service" (p. 19). The opportunity from Drucker's perspective is a situation that results from change occurring in one or more of the following areas (p. 35):

1. the unexpected-an unexpected success, failure, or outside event
2. an incongruity between reality as it actually is and reality as it is assumed to be or as it "ought to be";
3. innovation based on process need;
4. changes in industry structure or market structure that come about quickly and without warning;
5. demographics;
6. changes in perception, mood, and meaning; and
7. new knowledge.

The first four change areas originate with the entrepreneur or from within the firm (controllable), while the other three are environmental factors that lie outside the entrepreneur and firm (uncontrollable). Thus, an opportunity can be created or "manufactured" by the entrepreneur and/or may be created in the environment. To this end, researchers such as Christensen et al., (1994); Gaglio and Taub (1992); and Long and McMullan (1984) have developed opportunity recognition models that illustrate a confluence of factors, including both uncontrolled factors (e.g., cultural, social, economic and job forces, and personality) and controlled factors (e.g., alertness, job selection, study, moonlight venturing, and lifestyle). These factors affect the ability of a potential entrepreneur to recognize the opportunity and are described in greater detail in Chapter 3.

Drucker (1985) further argues that entrepreneurship can only take place when innovation occurs. According to Drucker, a person who opens a typical sandwich delicatessen is not an "entrepreneur" because there is nothing innovative about such a business other than the location. However, the founding and growth of McDonald's Corporation was "entrepreneurship" because the standardization of the food product and customer service, management and employee training, and quality standards allowed McDonald's to "drastically increase yield from resources, and created a new market and a new customer" (p. 22). Drucker's conception of entrepreneurial opportunity is therefore consistent with Schumpeter's, as it changes the equilibrium point of the market.

Vesper (1996) presents a broader view of opportunity and the role of innovation within entrepreneurship than that of Schumpeter and Drucker. While he agrees with Schumpeter and Drucker about the important role of innovation, he argues that, "Each new venture is an innovation. It, like a person, is individual" (p. 62). Vesper points out that although there may be great similarities between a new venture and existing businesses, subtle new differences in such factors as logos, decor, hours, prices, operating methods, and level of customer orientation are individualized and the success of the new venture may be determined by such differences. This Kirznerian conception of entrepreneurship recognizes the important incremental innovations of many business founders which result in major new profit creation. These individuals still assume risks and enter uncertain waters as they struggle to create firms and achieve success. A new venture may be highly profitable through slight differentiation from competitors, or by opening where there is no competition, but where a need exists.

Based on the differing views of "opportunity" by Kirzner, Schumpeter, Drucker, and Vesper, it may be seen that opportunities arise in different forms and degrees. Vesper (1993) integrates both the incremental (Kirzner) and radical transformational (Schumpeter/Drucker) conceptions in his concept of entrepreneurial opportunities. His broad definition describes an opportunity as a "gap" between the current state of affairs and some future, potentially improved state. The bridging of this gap is achieved through the functional actions and behaviors of entrepreneurs. Vesper also distinguishes between two specific types of opportunity: (1) a *business* opportunity, and (2) a *new venture* opportunity. The difference is that a *business opportunity* is one in which an entrepreneur within an established business recognizes an opportunity for new profit potential, while a *new venture opportunity* is one that can only be taken advantage of through the founding of an independent new venture. These distinctions are inclusive of both the incremental and radical conceptions of entrepreneurial opportunities.

Perhaps the most thorough and *specific* discussion of opportunities within the entrepreneurship literature comes from Timmons (1990; 1994a; 1994b; Timmons and Muzyka, 1994). He describes the qualities of an opportunity as being *attractive, durable,* and *timely,* and further, that opportunities must create or add value for the customer. According to Timmons (1994a), an opportunity can have these qualities only when the "window of opportunity" is opening, and when it remains open long enough for the entrepreneur to exploit the opportunity (see Figure 2).

Figure 2. Timmons' window of opportunity.

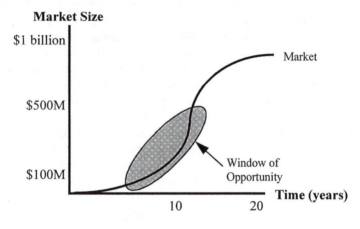

Figure 2 follows the typical product and industry life cycle curves (Kotler, 1991) and adapts it to a market life cycle. As a market begins to grow, the window of opportunity opens. Over time, the window begins to close as firms saturate the market. Thus, more opportunities exist early in a market life cycle, when product demand is growing (Hambrick and Lei, 1985; Hofer, 1975) and industry competition is not as intense as when the market matures and becomes saturated with competitors (Sandberg, 1986).

Timmons' argument is also supported in the population ecology literature by studies that plot population curves (e.g. Fichman and Levinthal, 1991; Singh et al., 1986; Utterback and Suárez, 1993), and in discussions of the carrying capacity of a population (Hannan and Freeman, 1977) and density dependence (e.g. Carroll and Hannan, 1989). Population ecologists have found that the growth rates and numbers of firms in a population is dependent on the life cycle stage of the industry. The numbers of firms in a population grow during the early stages of the industry, hit a maximum, and then begin to decline. Thus, the window of opportunity for most new ventures is during the initial growth stage of the industry life cycle.

As indicated in Figure 2, timing is often critical for successful opportunities to be recognized and taken advantage of, and early entrants may gain a competitive advantage as the numbers of opportunities increase during the early stages of market development; however, one does not have to be an early entrant to the market to recognize and exploit an opportunity. In fact, the window of opportunity never completely closes as long as the industry exists. Examples of successful new ventures that took on established competitors in mature markets include Southwest Airlines and *USA Today.*

Prior to Southwest Airlines, the airline industry was dominated by American, Delta, and United Airlines. Even with deregulation of the airline industry, the successful creation of another *national* competitor seemed unlikely given the industry structure and the enormous costs required to start an airline. Yet, Southwest has successfully captured a major share of the U.S. travel market and is continuing to grow at a rapid pace.

Also, few would have predicted the success of the daily national newspaper, *USA Today.* Prior to the newspaper's launch, local and regional newspapers and weekly news magazines enjoyed the loyalty of the newsreading public, but the Gannett Corporation persevered and reaped the benefits of its venture.

In a high growth industry without barriers to entry it may be easier, and even better, to simply enter the market, rather than undergo extensive strategic planning prior to new venture launch, because opportunities abound (Teach et. al, 1989). In such an industry, the population density is low (Hannan and Freeman, 1977), the carrying capacity of the industry is high (Carroll and Hannan, 1989), and there is no need to become a specialist (Lambkin, 1988; Romanelli, 1989). On the other hand, in mature industries entrepreneurial success can still be attained through selective screening and the identification of the "right" opportunities. For example, even in mature industries with significant barriers to entry, niche opportunities exist. Thus, while timing can be important, it is not always critical for opportunities to exist. This is further supported by the tendency for many good business opportunities to "lie dormant," waiting for someone to recognize and capitalize on them. In fact, it may be impossible to determine the proper timing before introducing some products or services. For example, the technology for such products as popcorn poppers, fiberglass skis, Post-It Notes®, and credit cards existed before these products came to market (Vesper, 1993), but time passed before they came to market. In such cases, the exact entry timing is not as important as the *act of introduction itself*. The market existed for Post-It Notes® and credit cards before and after they were introduced. *The opportunity in these cases had little to do with exact timing.*

Timmons' concept of opportunity does not define "opportunity" so much as what he (and most other people) perceives to be a "good" opportunity. His discussion is focused on the evaluation of opportunities (e.g., Timmons et al., 1987) and on the recognition of good opportunities from a strategic management perspective. The problem with this approach, with respect to the academic study of entrepreneurial opportunities, is that there is often an inverse relationship between market data and a potential entrepreneurial opportunity. Further, by using Timmons' framework, it would be difficult to identify opportunities in emerging industries due to little data being available to evaluate the potential success of such opportunities. Timmons' concept is more suited for opportunities which can be objectively evaluated using available information (Timmons and Muzyka, 1994). The Schumpeterian concept of opportunity, as a result of radical innovation, suggests that we should not limit our study to "good" opportunities because there may be no way to determine *a priori* if an opportunity is good or not. Using Timmons' definition of opportunities, it would be difficult to label the introduction of products such as "Baby on Board" signs, Tickle-Me-Elmo dolls, Rubik's Cubes, home computers, or the rapid growth of the Internet, entrepreneurial "opportunities" *prior* to their market introduction. Entrepreneurship scholars must, therefore, distinguish the elements of opportunity from the tangential issues related to opportunity.

It is easy to say that the timing was right for a product and/or that it was a good opportunity after it has made a significant amount of money. Van de Ven (1992) and Low and MacMillan (1988) point out that there are few longitudinal studies of the entrepreneurship process, and the use of retrospective case studies or archival data for empirical studies of entrepreneurship over time is problematic because bias can result when outcomes are known. The very use of the terms *attractive, durable, timely,* and *window of opportunity* can only be applied after the first movers have (1) developed a market and there is some data to support future opportunities, or (2) become successful. For example, it is unclear how the initial Federal Express concept would fit into Timmons' discussion of opportunity prior to firm founding.

Before Fred Smith conceived of the idea for an overnight delivery company, executives at UPS, Emery Air Freight, and the U.S. Postal Service had considered and rejected the idea because they perceived no market need for the service (Collins and Lazier, 1992). Smith recognized the opportunity and wrote a business plan for the company as an MBA class paper. He received a "C" in the class because his professor believed it was not feasible, although the plan was well written (Smith got an "A" for writing and style, and an "F" for feasibility for the plan). His professor and other potential competitors found Smith's idea was not attractive, durable, or timely, and was therefore not an opportunity. Had Smith not founded Federal Express, or if it had failed, from Timmons' concept of opportunity, it would have been tempting to dismiss the idea as not being an opportunity when in reality other factors could have caused the failure. Drucker (1985) points out that failures are rarely associated with "opportunities." Researchers must recognize that many firm failures occur *independently of opportunity*. Many failures are simply mistakes resulting from "greed, stupidity, thoughtless bandwagon-climbing, or incompetence whether in design or execution" (Drucker, 1985; p. 46).

For an opportunity to exist and be a construct capable of examination, it must be identifiable *before* the venture is founded and success is gained. Current conceptions of opportunity include other constructs and confounding variables, intertwined with the opportunity construct. As discussed above, we often make the mistake of requiring positive outcomes to certify that an entrepreneurial opportunity exists. While timing and the resources controlled are important factors when *evaluating* an opportunity, they are not required for an opportunity to exist. In many cases, the opportunity may be conceived and well developed before all the resources are acquired. Approximately 70 percent of both the *Inc.* 500 firms and firms that make up the National Federation of Independent Business database were founded with less than $50,000 of startup capital (see Vesper, 1996; p. 303). It may therefore be deduced that substantial resources are *not* necessary for an opportunity to exist. To conclude, for any type of predictive theoretical model or longitudinal study, entrepreneurship researchers cannot rely on hindsight to identify opportunities post hoc. Yet, from much of the existing literature, it is not possible to identify opportunities *a priori*.

2.3 IDEAS, DESIRABILITY, AND FEASIBILITY

Timmons (1990; 1994a; 1994b) points out that an "idea" for an entrepreneurial business does not necessarily equate to an "opportunity"-although the idea is always at the heart of an opportunity. Bygrave (1994; p. 13) adds that, "The idea per se is not what is important. In entrepreneurship, ideas really are a dime a dozen. Developing the idea, implementing it, and building a successful business are the important things." There is an important distinction between an idea and an opportunity. The distinction is that an opportunity is built upon the new venture idea-the idea is taken to another level. For example, opening an Indian restaurant in downtown Chicago may be a good *idea*. Yet, this is not an *entrepreneurial opportunity* because the founder may know nothing about the restaurant industry, or licenses and permits required to run a restaurant in Chicago. However, with research on the requirements of running a restaurant in Chicago, the idea of opening a restaurant can become an opportunity. Hence, the "idea" is a stepping stone that leads to an opportunity.

Entrepreneurship is a market driven process (Hills, 1994), and as Timmons (1990) points out, building a better mousetrap will not necessarily bring people to buy the new trap. Other factors must be considered for an idea to become an opportunity as potential customers must *want* the product. McMullan and Long (1990) state that an opportunity goes beyond a mental construct as it is determined by the physical and social reality. Without question, there is a social construction of reality (Berger and Luckmann, 1967). Human beings are social animals and many of our beliefs are largely dependent on social surroundings and develops out of our respective environments. As Granovetter (1994; p. 32) points out, human beings "do not behave or decide as atoms outside a social context, nor do they adhere slavishly to a script written for them by the particular intersection of sociocultural categories they happen to occupy. Their attempts at purposive action are instead embedded in concrete, ongoing systems of social relations." From this perspective, people's actions and beliefs are influenced by their positions within social networks, and social pressure can create the environmental conditions for opportunities to emerge. For example, survival does not depend on owning a fancy sports car or luxury automobile, yet for some upper class individuals there may be extreme peer pressure to do so. Upper class individuals may not want to be upstaged by their friends, and their social construction of reality may make owning an expensive car a necessity. At the same time, primitive tribes in South American rain forests place no value on luxury cars. In one environment, opportunity can exist to sell luxury cars, while in the other no such opportunity exists.

As noted earlier, according to Stevenson et al. (1989), an opportunity is more of a "situation." And further, for a situation to be a good opportunity, it must be feasible and it must represent a desirable future state (Christensen et al., 1994). Christensen and his associates (1994) point out that "feasible" refers to technical and economic factors, while "desirable" is subjective. The example of the expensive car illustrates the importance of the potential entrepreneur's frame of reference and social reality to his/her conception of what is feasible and desirable. However, feasibility should not be limited to the economic connotation which is often the primary focus of *feasibility studies*. Rather, utilizing a broader definition of feasibility, for an opportunity to exist it must be possible. Offering potential customers trips to the moon by teleporting them instantaneously to the lunar surface could be a good business. It could cater to a very wealthy clientele and charge millions of dollars for each trip. But the technology does not currently exist for teleportation. Because this particular service idea is impossible to deliver it is not an opportunity so much as a visionary idea (or foolish musing, depending on your perspective).

Again, not all opportunities are desirable or feasible for every potential founder; however, from an objective standpoint, an opportunity can only be considered an opportunity when the benefits of bridging the gap between the actual state and the potentially improved state outweigh the costs of doing so (Vesper, 1993). In other words, if a positive return on investment cannot be achieved and it costs more to take advantage of the perceived opportunity than it does to remain status quo, then the perceived opportunity is not really an opportunity. The pursuit of such an "opportunity" would be a foolhardy exercise rather than the pursuit of an actual opportunity.

Caution must be exercised by entrepreneurship researchers who consider feasibility and desirability. Some of the most innovative opportunities are those that cannot be evaluated because they are so new and it may not be possible to fully appreciate the full potential of such opportunities. Even an idea such as the moon tour business may become a feasible and desirable opportunity with the discovery of a new form of technology and with an appropriate entrepreneur in a supportive social and economic setting.

2.4 ENVIRONMENTAL SOURCES OF OPPORTUNITY CREATION

Earlier in the chapter, Drucker's (1985) sources of opportunity were summarized. Adding, and to some degree overlapping with Drucker's discussion, Stevenson and Gumpert (1985) described not *what* an opportunity is, but *where it exists*. According to Stevenson and Gumpert, four external pressures lead to opportunities. These include rapid changes in: (1) technology, (2) consumer economics, (3) social values, and (4) political action and regulatory standards which affect competition.

2.4.1 Technology

Throughout the course of history, new technologies have emerged and replaced older technologies. Often, improved technology is the means by which businesses can produce goods or provide services that are better, faster, and/or cheaper. As such, technological changes can give rise to new forms of profit potential.

Perhaps not coincidentally, the growth in firm foundings in recent years has paralleled the growing power and affordability of computer and information technologies. Robust information technologies that were once reserved for cash-rich corporations and government entities have become available to smaller firms and individuals. The Internet and e-mail are now increasingly making physical location obsolete. For example, products and services can be sold to customers all over the world through a World Wide Web site. And the cost of maintaining a Web site and marketing over the Internet is minimal compared to normal channels (newspapers, magazines, radio, TV, direct mail, etc.). These rapid changes in technology have created new opportunities for entrepreneurship by significantly improving operations and making it possible for smaller competitors to carve out niche markets from larger market dominators.

2.4.2. Consumer Economics

Changes in economic conditions may force consumers to reevaluate how they spend their money. For example, there are differences in consumers' spending patterns during recessions as compared to periods of economic booms. These changes can greatly impact the numbers and types of opportunities that exist.

An example of opportunity created by rapid changes in consumer economics can be seen by the effects of stagflation and the oil embargo of the 1970s on the auto industry. The embargo dramatically increased the price of gasoline to record levels as supplies ran scarce. Long lines at gas stations and economic concerns changed consumer preferences from traditional larger cars produced by the Big Three (Chrysler, General Motors, and Ford) in the United States to smaller, more economical Japanese imports. The Big Three were slow to react and Japanese auto manufacturers took advantage of the opportunity by claiming huge chunks of market share.

2.4.3. Social Values

As time passes, customer preferences and what is considered socially desirable change. What is "in" one year may be "out" the next as tastes change. For example, the fitness craze that overwhelmed America in the 1980s exemplifies opportunities created through changing social values. The abundant number of companies that have been created to offer exercise equipment are the direct result of the American population's obsession with fitness.

2.4.4. Political Action and Regulatory Standards

Changes in the political arena and to regulations can create entire industries. For example, the creation of the Environmental Protection Agency (EPA), and the passage of environmental legislation in the 1970s created a booming environmental consulting and remediation industry. Import tariff reductions can make overseas manufacturing more attractive. Sweeping political action and reform such as the breakup of AT&T and the deregulation of the telecommunications industry has made it possible for new, smaller phone companies and wireless service providers to compete in what was once a monopolistic market.

2.4.5. Other Environmental Sources

In addition to the four major issues above, Vesper (1993) points out that changes in *demographics,* or *natural disasters* and *resource discoveries* may add to the number of opportunities available to would-be entrepreneurs. For example the aging U.S. population has created a larger need for nursing care and home medical equipment and the growing Hispanic population has created an industry for Hispanic television and radio stations. Natural disasters such as Mt. St. Helen's eruption and the San Francisco earthquake, led to the creation of tourism companies and numerous construction and clean up firms, respectively. And, the discovery of new oil reserves in Alaska has borne out new construction and mining firms (Vesper, 1993).

These are some of the major environmental factors which can create opportunities. However, the potential for the opportunity, as supported in the environment, does not necessarily mean that potential business founders will recognize the opportunity. The capabilities and life experiences of the individual entrepreneur are still required to recognize the opportunity. This is discussed in greater detail in the following chapter.

2.5 A CONCEPTUAL DEFINITION OF OPPORTUNITY

An opportunity is a construct that results from factors that are both within the control of the entrepreneur (e.g., background, experience) and outside the control of the entrepreneur (contextual and environmental factors). It may represent an incremental innovation (Kirznerian) or a radical innovation (Schumpeterian) to the market. The largest challenge in defining opportunity is in making the distinctions of where the idea ends, the opportunity begins, and where the development of the business concept and acquisition of the required resources takes place. After the opportunity is identified, the actual business concept can be developed and resources acquired to take advantage of the opportunity. This conception of a linear process separates the new venture idea from the opportunity and, further, the opportunity from the acquisition of required resources and the actual business formation. Thus, the opportunity is conceptually discrete, separate from other parts of the entrepreneurship process.

It is proposed that an *entrepreneurial opportunity* is a feasible, profit-seeking, potential venture that provides an innovative new product or service to the market, improves on an existing product/service, or imitates a profitable product/service in a less-than-saturated market. From this definition an entrepreneurial opportunity may provide an innovative new product/service that creates its own market (creates new supply and demand curve), or it may provide an improvement on an existing product/service (moves demand curve), or provide a similar alternative to an existing product or service in a growing market (moves supply curve).

Some further clarification is needed on the terms within the definition given above. First, non-profit organizations are excluded from the definition. An entrepreneurial opportunity must have profit potential and offer some improvement to the market, either by making transformational or incremental changes, or by helping to fill unmet needs. It may represent an improvement for all actors in the market - the entrepreneur, clients, suppliers, creditors - or just some of them. Second, "venture" refers to a "speculative business enterprise" (*Merriam-Webster Dictionary*, 1989; p. 805). Within the entrepreneurship literature, ventures are often considered synonymous with "firms." Newly formed firms are new ventures; however, a venture can also be a new division within an existing firm, or a combination of two or more firms (i.e., joint venture), which provides new products or services (Lumpkin and Dess, 1996). Finally, to reiterate, "feasible" is used in the broadest sense of the word. Being feasible means that the potential venture is possible (i.e., does not break the laws of physics) and permissible under the law.

Throughout the chapter, the role of contextual and environmental factors which lead to opportunity has been discussed, but the relationship between the entrepreneur and the opportunity is also important. From a practical point of view, the entrepreneur who recognizes the opportunity must be included in any conception of opportunity because if no one recognizes the opportunity it really does not matter if the opportunity exists. Undiscovered opportunities are impossible to know and impossible to study. Further, for one person, a set of circumstances may provide an opportunity, where for others there may be no opportunity. Much depends on the individual, his/her knowledge and experiences, social context, and expectations for the future. For all intents and purposes, the entrepreneurial opportunity cannot be separated from the entrepreneur.

Thus, an entrepreneurial opportunity is derived from three factors: (1) the personal knowledge, abilities, and background of the entrepreneur, (2) the new venture idea itself, and (3) environmental variables (i.e., regulatory issues, economic conditions). Equation 2-1 represents the relationship between opportunity and these three factors.

$$O = f(P, I, E) \tag{2-1}$$

where: O = Entrepreneurial Opportunity
       P = Personal Knowledge, Abilities, and Background of the Entrepreneur
       I = New Venture Idea
       E = Environmental Variables

The new venture idea is central to opportunity (Timmons, 1990; 1994a; 1994b); however, the environment must support the potential opportunity and the different abilities and backgrounds of individual entrepreneurs will yield different potential opportunities. Only when all three factors fit together will the circumstances exist for the entrepreneurial opportunity to be revealed. Thus, an entrepreneurial opportunity is borne out of the combination of forces illustrated in Figure 3. The new venture idea is influenced by both the entrepreneur and the environment, and a reciprocal relationship exists between the entrepreneur and the environment. Unrecognized opportunities exist all around us, but it takes the right person, in the right environment to develop a new venture idea that can result in a "recognized" entrepreneurial opportunity.

As discussed earlier in the chapter, opportunity is independent of resources controlled and may not be dependent on timing. While timing and resources controlled can make an opportunity more attractive and improve the chances for success, they are not necessary for an opportunity to exist. When opportunities arise, entrepreneurs can seek to secure the resources necessary to take

Figure 3. The entrepreneurial opportunity.

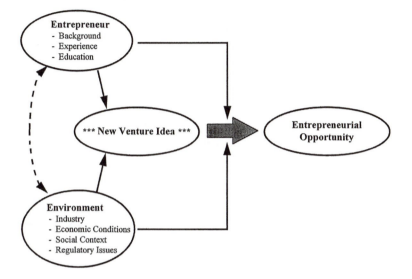

advantage of them. Opportunities rely on innovation, which can be either incremental (i.e., Kirzner, 1973; 1979) or transformational (Drucker, 1985; Schumpeter, 1934). Also, entrepreneurial opportunities may target small, niche markets, or broad markets. This chapter is provided to help better understand what the qualities of an opportunity are, and where they come from; the next chapter builds on this one by examining how entrepreneurs *recognize* opportunities.

CHAPTER 3

Opportunity Recognition Literature Review

3.1 CHAPTER 3 INTRODUCTION

In Chapter 2, a conceptual discussion and definition of opportunity was provided. This chapter summarizes the existing opportunity recognition literature. While there is some overlap between the two chapters, this chapter focuses on the theories and findings related to *recognition*.

From a strategic management perspective, we would expect that firms in the marketplace would constantly be scanning the environment (Thompson and Strickland, 1992) or analyzing competitive forces (Porter, 1979) to identify opportunities. Then, once identified, existing firms would take advantage of the opportunities. However, Vesper (1993) describes three reasons why many established companies fail to take advantage of opportunities in their industry:

1. Nobody in the company that should have exploited the opportunity thought of it, or
2. Somebody thought of it, but the company declined to go after it, or
3. The company did decide to go after it but did not do so effectively.

Stevenson and Gumpert (1985) argue that for an opportunity to be recognized, one must have an external (market) orientation rather than an internal (resource) orientation. They further point out that this type of orientation - one that constantly looks to find innovation and the pursuit of opportunity - is difficult for executives in established firms because change can be painful. Internal processes become institutionalized (Meyer and Rowan, 1977; Powell and DiMaggio, 1991) and structural inertia builds up over time (Hannan and Freeman, 1977). The uncertainty that goes with an external orientation is difficult for many executives because there is a comfort level and sense of security that comes with the predictability of stable environments.

The Schumpeterian and Kirznerian conceptions of the entrepreneur as the market innovator highlight the importance of entrepreneurs to society. They rejuvenate the economy by improving products and services. Further, successful entrepreneurs are examples of individuals who have managed to overcome concerns about uncertainty and developed the external orientation needed to recognize opportunities. But how entrepreneurs recognize opportunities is still unknown, for as Timmons (1990) points out, if it were so easy someone who wanted to start a business would just have to pick up one of the many available checklists and idea generators (e.g., Vesper, 1996; p. 60–61). Realizing that there are so few successful entrepreneurs and so little is known about how and why they recognize the opportunities for their businesses, opportunity recognition becomes a critical area for entrepreneurship scholars to research.

Inherently, good entrepreneurial opportunities must be practical and McMullan and Long (1990; p. 269) propose that opportunity identification is "the challenge of transforming a vision of 'what might be' into a vision of 'what can be'." Clearly, this is a sweeping, although rather diffuse, definition of opportunity recognition. Before going any further, it is important to extend the discussion of *opportunities* from the last chapter by more precisely defining *opportunity recognition*. Based primarily on the definition offered by Christensen et al., (1989), recognizing an opportunity is perceiving a possibility for new profit potential through (a) the founding and formation of a new venture or b) the significant improvement of an existing venture. From this broad definition, opportunity recognition can be conceived of as an activity that can occur both prior to firm founding and after firm founding throughout the life of the firm.

Again, not much is known about how entrepreneurs identify opportunities (Hills, 1995; Stasch, 1990); however, there is a small, but growing, body of opportunity recognition literature that addresses this important research area. The remainder of this chapter reviews what we know about entrepreneurial opportunity recognition.

3.2 OPPORTUNITY RECOGNITION: PROCESS OR ENLIGHTENMENT?

Entrepreneurs are widely considered to be attracted to risky ventures that promise above average profit and growth (d'Amboise and Muldowney, 1988). They are often conceived of as unconventional, unique, and innovative in their approach to business and the market (e.g., Schumpeter, 1934). Conventional academic thought is that systematic search (Vesper, 1980) and/or careful strategic planning is needed to identify opportunities (Timmons et al., 1987). However, Hills (1996) found that formal customer surveys and market analyses were not considered as important as "gut feel" to entrepreneurs when it came to evaluating opportunities. This belief in informality may also be true when it comes to identifying opportunities; formal search for ideas may not be the method of choice for all entrepreneurs.

In a study of software firms, Teach et al. (1989) found different styles of opportunity recognition among the software firm presidents studied. Only about half favored systematic approaches to searching for opportunities. In addition, perhaps to the chagrin of academic scholars of strategy and management, Teach and his colleagues also reported that firms founded on venture ideas that were "accidentally" discovered and which had not been subjected to formal screening achieved break-even sales faster than those firms that had undergone more formal search and planning techniques. It should be noted that the importance of formal search and planning to subsequent survival and performance is likely to be moderated by such things as industry maturity and barriers to entry. As discussed in the previous chapter, in mature industries with significant barriers to entry, careful planning and formal evaluation of opportunities may be critical to success, whereas in a high growth industry without barriers to entry it may be better to just jump into opportunities because the carrying capacity of the industry is high and there is no need to become a specialist (Carroll and Hannan, 1989; Lambkin, 1988; Romanelli, 1989). The software companies analyzed by Teach et al. (1989) represent firms in a growing industry and results may have been different if the researchers had looked at firms in a more mature industry.

Timmons (1990; 1994a; 1994b) takes a strategic approach to opportunity recognition, describing it as a screening and evaluation activity that takes business ideas and weeds out good opportunities. Some authors such as McMullan and Long (1990); Stevenson et al. (1989); and Vesper (1996) present discovery questions and checklists in their entrepreneurship textbooks that can help potential entrepreneurs identify opportunities. From their perspective, entrepreneurial opportunity recognition can be achieved through systematic search. While this may be true, there are many entrepreneurs who do not undergo a formal search for opportunities, instead they recognize a need and create an organization to fulfill it (Bhave, 1994; Cyert and March, 1963). On a related note, strategic search and planning may not yield a better opportunity (Teach et al., 1989). Drucker (1985) gives other examples of failed products such as the Ford Edsel and padlocks in India that were extensively researched prior to market introduction.

Hills (1996) compared the responses of a group of highly successful entrepreneurs (n = 53) to a representative sample of entrepreneurs (n = 187) on a variety of opportunity recognition items. Over 85 percent of both groups indicated that identifying opportunities was several learning steps over time, rather than a one-time occurrence. Additionally, over 80 percent of both groups reported that the consideration of one opportunity led to other opportunities. This would seem to indicate that opportunity recognition is a process with intermediate steps, rather than the one-time cognitive breakthrough resulting from an enlightenment experience.

Some researchers have attempted to develop conceptual models of the opportunity recognition process (Bhave, 1994; Christensen et al., 1994; Gaglio and Taub, 1992; Long and McMullan, 1984). For the most part, these attempts have not told us much about the types of opportunities that are recognized and/or why entrepreneurs choose to pursue one opportunity over another, but they have described critical steps in the process. As Gaglio and Taub (1992) point out, most researchers describe opportunity recognition as a linear process. Gaglio and Taub summarize existing literature on the typical process as having four major steps: (1) the Pre-recognition Stew, (2) the Eureka! Experience, (3) the Development of the Idea, and (4) the Decision to Proceed.

According to Gaglio and Taub (1992), entrepreneurial opportunity recognition occurs based on a number of factors, including market demands, personal attributes, social forces, technology, etc. Once the opportunity is recognized by the entrepreneur in the "Eureka!" stage of the process, the opportunity is further developed and issues related to the market including required resources are considered. The model implies that once a determination is made regarding the feasibility and desirability of the opportunity, the decision to proceed with, or abort the opportunity is made by the entrepreneur.

Christensen et al. (1994) also developed a linear model of the opportunity recognition process. Their model highlights the importance of *desirability* and *feasibility* as antecedents to the identification of the opportunity. The central role of these two characteristics, as well as the placement of "formal strategic planning" at the end of the model are evidence that these authors were influenced by the work of Stevenson and his associates (1985; 1986; 1989; summarized in the last chapter).

Unlike Gaglio and Taub (1992), Christensen et al. (1994) specify individual factors that lead to opportunity recognition, rather than combining all of the factors into one large conglomeration. These factors are separated into four categories which may be both within and outside the control of the entrepreneur. More specifically, entrepreneurs can control the Firm Specific Factors, Management Behavior, and Strategic Thinking, while Environmental Factors lie outside their control. In addition, in contrast with the model summarized by Gaglio and Taub, Christensen and his colleagues argue that the assessment of desirability and feasibility must occur *before* the opportunity is identified. This is a major departure from the model presented by Gaglio and Taub, who viewed these to be part of the evaluation stage of the process (after the opportunity has been recognized).

Christensen et al. (1994) discuss feasibility and desirability as important factors for opportunity. Feasibility is contained explicitly within the definition at the end of Chapter 2 and desirability is based on social context and individual characteristics (see Figure 3).

An opportunity that is not feasible and desirable cannot exist. For example, an individual may recognize that a particular urban neighborhood needs a dry cleaner. The potential entrepreneur may have access to lease space and the knowledge required to open the business (feasibility) but may not want to work the long hours or with the toxic chemicals (not desirable). In this case, the business idea was identified but it never developed into an opportunity. Entrepreneurship researchers must recognize this subtle distinction between idea and opportunity.

Long and McMullan (1984) describe the opportunity recognition process as being at least partially under the control of the entrepreneur. They argue that in order for an opportunity to become realizable, a significant amount of preparation is required. And it is this preparation that "personalizes" the opportunity making it inaccessible to most other people.

The Long and McMullan (1984) model parallels the Gaglio and Taub (1992) summary model and the Christensen et al. (1994) model. A confluence of factors, including both uncontrolled factors (cultural, social, economic and job forces, and personality) and controlled factors (alertness, job selection, study, moonlight venturing, and lifestyle), affect the ability of a potential entrepreneur to recognize the opportunity, and the evaluation and elaboration phase (strategic planning) occurs after the recognition of the opportunity. However, Long and McMullan provide a more refined discussion and analysis of the factors which lead to opportunity recognition. The ten antecedents to the actual opportunity recognition stage demonstrate the breadth of factors-both within the entrepreneur's control and outside his/her control-which can impact the recognition process. Through these factors, an individual can have what Long and McMullan (1984) call an 'aha' experience when the opportunity is recognized. Afterwards, the opportunity is elaborated and evaluated before a decision about whether to proceed is made. During the elaboration stage, the opportunity may be honed and modified to better fit the market and to maximize the profit potential.

Bhave (1994) also proposed a process model of venture creation with opportunity recognition being the key early stage in the sequence of events leading to the creation of the venture. Using an open-ended interview technique, Bhave surveyed 27 New York City firms in an effort to better understand the venture creation process. The firms in his sample represented four major industries (trade and distribution, financial and management consulting, computer services, and technology based design and manufacturing). Perhaps his most important contribution to the literature was his identification and illustration of two different types of opportunity recognition based on Cyert and March's (1963) earlier typology which divided opportunity recognition into two categories: externally stimulated and internally stimulated opportunity recognition.

An externally stimulated opportunity is one where the decision to start a venture precedes opportunity recognition. Entrepreneurs who recognize the opportunities for their businesses through this process engage in an ongoing search for opportunities which they filter, massage, and elaborate before founding their firms. An alternative venture creation path results from internally stimulated opportunity recognition. Here the entrepreneurs discover problems to solve or needs to fulfill and only later decide to create ventures. Bhave's opportunity recognition model highlights the fact that opportunities can result from different processes.

Bhave's (1994) model describes two primary processes that lead to the venture formation. In the first path, the externally stimulated opportunity recognition path, the entrepreneur makes a conscious decision to start a business, searches for and recognizes opportunities, then chooses one to create a business. An example of this type of entrepreneur is Barry Potekin, the founder of Gold Coast Dogs in Chicago. Over a 15 year period during the 1970s and early 1980s, Mr. Potekin had built and lost a fortune as a real estate agent and precious metals investor. He went from having a million dollar home on Chicago's North Shore to living in a friend's apartment because he could not afford to rent an apartment on his own. Under financial strain, he made a conscious decision to change his life and rebuild his fortune through entrepreneurship. With the motivation and drive but no idea, he brainstormed at the kitchen table in his parent's home. After considering a variety of businesses, he decided to open a restaurant. He went on to found Gold Coast Dogs, a fast food restaurant specializing in Chicago hot dogs. His business has prospered and he has been able to gain local and national press (including *Wall Street Journal*, CNN, CBS News, *Chicago Tribune, Chicago Sun-Times*) for his riches-to-rags-and-back-to-riches story, and his innovative marketing and management style (IES, 1994).

The second path illustrates the process of internally stimulated opportunity recognition. In this case, a formal search is not used to recognize an opportunity, rather a need is recognized and fulfilled. The opportunity develops out of the recognition of a potential new venture. This is in sharp contrast to the externally stimulated opportunity which is the culmination of a formal search process. Shari Whitley, CEO of Women's Workout World, exemplifies this type of entrepreneur. After years of working as an aerobics instructor in the health club industry, she saw the growing trend in health and fitness and recognized the need for a high quality women's health club. She bought out Women's Workout World, a small struggling chain of fitness clubs for women, improved the equipment and services, and raised membership fees. Under her direction and leadership, the organization has grown rapidly. It has nearly doubled revenues in the five years since Ms. Whitley took over and is now a $12,000,000/year business (IES, 1996)

From the two examples above and the discussion of Bhave's (1994) model, opportunity recognition can occur through two very different processes. In one there is a conscious search for the opportunity (externally stimulated, i.e., Barry Potekin), and the other seems to be more of an "accidental" process as a need is identified and the opportunity emerges (internally stimulated; i.e., Shari Whitley). The externally stimulated opportunity recognition process is consistent with Vesper's (1980) discussion of systematic search and Timmons perspective on opportunities. While both internally and externally stimulated opportunities are important, little empirical research has examined the difference between the two, and further study is needed.

In addition to the distinction between internally versus externally stimulated opportunities, an interesting and important contribution is the filtration and the refinement that takes place before the business concept is identified. Bhave (1994) defines the business concept as a fully refined opportunity. The model indicates that opportunity recognition does not occur through a discrete linear process. Rather, a "simmering" effect takes place as a variety of opportunities are examined before one is selected as the formal business concept. The concepts of time and consideration of multiple opportunities before an opportunity is selected are important features of the model. The development of ideas into entrepreneurial opportunities may require numerous improvements and go through a number of revisions. And further, the time required for the developmental steps required to turn ideas into opportunities will differ depending on the type of opportunity, the environment, and the entrepreneur. Time within the opportunity recognition process is not a constant. For some entrepreneurs the recognition of the idea and opportunity may be simultaneous, while others may take weeks, days, and even years before recognizing their opportunity from a new venture idea.

The process models discussed above illustrate some of the factors which can lead to opportunity recognition. Several of them either explicitly or implicitly include individual differences between people as being a factor. Personal characteristics and just starting a new venture and being in the marketplace can lead to opportunities. These issues are discussed in the next two sections.

3.3 PRIOR EXPERIENCE AND THE "CORRIDOR PRINCIPLE"

Entrepreneurship is a market driven phenomenon (Hills, 1994) and market demand is one antecedent to opportunity recognition. Yet, one cannot rely solely on market demand to predict opportunity recognition, because in many cases the demand for a product is not explicit, particularly in the case of innovative new products which may be unknown to customers prior to introduction. However, having personal experience and knowledge of an industry may allow an entrepreneur to recognize market gaps and assess the market potential of a new venture.

Prior research has shown that personal experience in an industry leads many entrepreneurs to their venture ideas (Vesper, 1996). A 1989 survey of the *Inc.* 500 founders revealed that 43 percent got the idea for their venture while working in the same industry (Case, 1989). This percentage is consistent with another survey of 2,994 members of the National Federation of Independent Businesses (Cooper et al., 1990). While working in another firm, an individual may learn how to operate within the industry and/or see a market niche that is unserved. Using the knowledge and experience gained, the entrepreneur can found a venture. In addition, it is possible that discussions with industry contacts and business associates may lead to opportunities. The specific role of entrepreneurs' social networks is discussed later in this chapter and in Chapter 4.

Simply working in an industry may lead to opportunities that would not be seen if the entrepreneur had not founded a firm. In other words, entrepreneurs may discover ideas by just "muddling through" their day-to-day business operations. According to Ronstadt's (1988) Corridor Principle, once entrepreneurs found their firms they begin a journey down a corridor, and as they proceed through the corridor, windows of opportunity open up around them. The key point is that entrepreneurs would not see these opportunities if they had not entered the corridor (i.e., founded their firm and entered the marketplace). Hills (1996) found indirect support for the Corridor Principle, noting that entrepreneurs reported that "immersion" in an industry was needed to identify opportunities and that the consideration of one opportunity often led to other opportunities. In addition, an overwhelming majority (approximately 95 percent) of surveyed entrepreneurs agreed that, once in the market, they must be prepared to change their product or service based on changes in the market. Thus, opportunity recognition is an ongoing process that continues throughout the life of the organization and may even be fostered by firm founding and working in an industry.

Christensen and Peterson (1990) examined the sources of new venture ideas using four structured case field studies with fifteen ventures and a survey of 76 companies. They concluded that specific problems and social encounters are often a source of venture ideas, but also that profound market or technological knowledge is a prerequisite for venture ideas. Thus, personal experience is the only way to develop market knowledge. Further, being in the marketplace and knowing the day-to-day operations and seeing the needs of customers first-hand can help an entrepreneur recognize potential opportunities. Yet, many people have industry experience but never found their own firms and become entrepreneurs. They may lack the propensity for risk taking (Brockhaus, 1980; Brockhaus and Horwitz, 1986), or perhaps they simply do not recognize the opportunity. The latter is explored in the next section.

3.4 COGNITIVE FACTORS FOR OPPORTUNITY RECOGNITION

Do successful entrepreneurs have a "sixth" sense that allows them to recognize opportunities? We know that in some cases the opportunity for a business, product, or service may have been waiting to be discovered for a long time before it was introduced to the market (Vesper, 1993). It is possible that entrepreneurs have what Kirzner (1973; 1979) describes as entrepreneurial "alertness." Research has shown that entrepreneurs often perceive themselves to be alert to opportunities (Hills, 1996; Hills et al., 1997), but are entrepreneurs more sensitive to opportunity? Studying this question forces us to delve into the cognitive differences debate that has proven to be inconclusive (see Low and MacMillan, 1988) and even vilified by some (Gartner, 1988; 1990).

Based on Kirzner's (1973; 1979) work, Kaish and Gilad (1991) searched for differences between entrepreneurs and managers in terms of entrepreneurial alertness. The researchers compared 51 company founders with 36 executives in a large company and found that entrepreneurs scan their environment for new business opportunities, while managers tend to rely on more traditional economic analyses to determine the feasibility of an opportunity. In addition, entrepreneurs spent more time searching for information on their own time and used different information sources than executives including paying special attention to cues about the risks of new opportunities. As argued by Kaish and Gilad, this would support the idea that alertness is a special characteristic of entrepreneurs.

Similarly, Gaglio and Taub (1992), examined whether the concept of entrepreneurial alertness is a unique cognitive skill of entrepreneurs. Using a sample of business owners and corporate managers, they presented the two groups with an ambiguous business situation and asked respondents to search for new business opportunities or ideas. Again, the researchers found that the two groups approached the task differently. However, while their results were supportive of the alertness construct, Gaglio and Taub's (1992) study was exploratory and they cautioned against using their findings as evidence of alertness on the part of entrepreneurs.

There is little empirical research on alertness. As Busenitz (1996) points out, Kaish and Gilad's (1991) study had several methodological limitations which call their findings into question. They used small sample sizes, had low reliabilities between some of their scale items (below the normally accepted .70 alpha), and used a comparative sample of managers from only one organization. In addition, the generalizability of their results is in question because they used a non-random sample of entrepreneurs who were government contractors. Further, Busenitz (1996) replicated Kaish and Gilad's work using a random sample of entrepreneurs and managers from many different firms, and found little support for Kaish and Gilad's original finding. Rather than dismiss Kaish and Gilad's findings, Busenitz argued for the development and refinement of measures of entrepreneurial alertness.

Thus, the mixed empirical findings described above leave us without definitive support for the alertness construct. Based on the limited number of studies, further examination is needed to support or refute the alertness hypothesis.

3.5 SOCIAL NETWORKS AND OPPORTUNITY RECOGNITION

As indicated earlier in the chapter, social encounters are often a source of venture ideas (Christensen and Peterson, 1990), and thus, can lead to opportunity recognition. However, there is little research on this important subject. Theories about the importance of weak ties (Granovetter, 1973) and structural holes (Burt, 1992) may shed light on the importance of social networks to opportunity recognition and differences in the types of opportunities identified.

In his classic paper on the strength of weak ties, Granovetter (1973) argues that weak ties act as "bridges" to information sources not contained within an individual's immediate (strong-tie) network. Based on Granovetter's (1973) discussion, the casual acquaintance is more likely to provide unique information than are close friends because most people have many more weak ties than they do strong ties and there are many access points between the individual and his strong ties (i.e., if one friend does not reveal information another one will). In contrast, there is usually only one connection to a weak tie and thus only one connection to the information. Burt's (1992) work on "structural holes" follows a rationale similar to the weak ties argument. He argues that it is not the strength of the relationship between network ties that predicts access to unique information, but rather the "spaces" between network relationships. Defining the space between nonredundant contacts as "structural holes," he shows the potential benefits and importance of the holes within a network. These concepts are discussed in greater detail in the next chapter.

Koller (1988) studied the sources of new venture ideas. He surveyed 65 entrepreneurs in several industries and found that half reported their ideas had come through social contacts. The other half had recognized their businesses individually. Further, he found significant differences in the types of opportunities identified between the two groups. More specifically, those who came up with the ideas themselves were more likely to use prior experience and be motivated out of a "desire for entrepreneurship" than those who got their ideas from their social network. In addition, less than 25 percent of his sample had no experience in their firm's industry prior to founding. Combining the fact that Koller's results indicate that both experience in the industry and network sources are important, we might speculate that industry experience can be an important way for an entrepreneur to expand his/her business network, and thus, access to information.

In an exploratory paper on the importance of social networks to opportunity recognition, Hills et al. (1997) found significant differences between "solo entrepreneurs" (those who identified their business idea alone) and "network entrepreneurs" (those who did not develop their business idea alone) on a number of different issues. Among the findings, the researchers found that network entrepreneurs identified significantly more opportunities than solo entrepreneurs, but were less likely to describe themselves as being opportunistic, as having special alertness or sensitivity to opportunities, or as being creative. Solo entrepreneurs were significantly more likely to set aside time to be creative, and were more likely to go through a formal search. They also reported that prior employment and "immersion" in an industry are needed to identify opportunities. Network entrepreneurs, on the other hand, believed that it was easier to see real opportunities after entering a market. These findings hint at some of the important differences between the two types of entrepreneurs. Network entrepreneurs learned of more opportunities than solo entrepreneurs and took advantage of opportunities in which they had no direct experience. They were more likely to take advantage of opportunities in industries that they were not "immersed" in or did not have personal experience than were solo entrepreneurs. The authors hypothesized that network entrepreneurs used their network contacts to provide feasible, solid opportunities and could defer to the personal expertise and experience of their contact(s) to reduce uncertainty. Based on the findings of the study, it is possible that network entrepreneurs do not have to be as engaged in search activities or be as creative as solo entrepreneurs because they have access to a wider range of information and creativity through network ties.

While their results are interesting and open a door for a new path of research. A key limitation of the study is the use of a single measure item to distinguish between solo and network entrepreneurs. The authors reported that they chose to move ahead with the single item measure for three reasons: (1) it was an exploratory study; (2) there was a 50/50 breakdown of network vs. solo entrepreneurs which was consistent with Koller's (1988) finding; and (3) the results were consistent with social network theory. They concluded by calling for the use of multi-item measures to distinguish network entrepreneur from solo entrepreneurs.

3.6 CONCEPT OF THE OPPORTUNITY RECOGNITION PROCESS IN THIS STUDY

It is important to make the conception of the opportunity recognition process used in this study clear. Recognizing an opportunity is perceiving a possibility for new profit potential through (a) the founding and formation of a new venture or b) the significant improvement of an existing venture (Christensen et al., 1989). Further, it should be noted that opportunity recognition *is a process* and that it can occur both prior to firm founding and after firm founding throughout the life of the firm. Based on prior research, opportunity recognition is not a "Eureka" experience (Hills, 1996), although it is possible that it can be in rare instances.

This study follows the basic steps of the Long and McMullan (1984) process model of opportunity recognition (shown earlier in this chapter). Their model illustrates both the idea (initial vision) and the opportunity (elaborated vision), although they do not explicitly use the term "idea." The differences between ideas and opportunities were discussed in the prior chapter (Bygrave, 1994; Timmons, 1990; 1994a; 1994b). When we take a closer look at the Long and McMullan (1984) model, we find that they describe the "aha" experience as "identifying the field of opportunity." This could be considered the idea generation and then opportunity recognition would take place after what they describe is the "Strategic Idea Elaboration" process.

Any model of opportunity recognition should distinguish between new venture ideas and opportunities. By paring down the opportunity recognition process to its most basic form, we are left with the model illustrated in Figure 4. Based on that model, we can see that an entrepreneur could come up with initial new venture *ideas* and after some additional thought and/or evaluation, they may recognize that their ideas are potential new venture *opportunities*. With even further thought and consideration one may then decide to start a new venture.

The three steps shown above are consistent with the definitions of opportunity and opportunity recognition provided earlier, as well as Long and McMullan's (1984) model. This simple model can be a powerful tool in the study of opportunity recognition because it offers a theoretical framework which provides guidance to survey subjects or interviewees. It can be presented to a study subject quickly and easily before any questions on opportunity recognition are asked. As discussed in the last chapter, the definition of opportunities has not been consistent in published research and as such it is difficult to compare between studies. Using this model, a researcher can help ensure that research subjects understand that there is a difference between ideas and opportunities.

3.7 DISCUSSION AND CONCLUDING REMARKS

Opportunity recognition is the trigger that sets the entrepreneurship process in motion, but little is known about how and why it happens. When one thinks about how many people live out their lives following the beaten paths of others, it would appear that most fail to recognize their opportunity(ies). There is a saying which warns that *opportunity knocks, but once*; in fact, the poem at

Figure 4. Basic steps of the opportunity recognition process.

the beginning of Chapter 2 hits upon that very point. If this were true, it would imply that few opportunities exist; however, based on the discussion throughout this chapter, it is quite possible that some individuals have the potential for more opportunities than others (i.e., opportunity knocks more than once).

Jack Goeken exemplifies a person who has benefited from having numerous opportunities come his way. Over a 30 year period, Mr. Goeken founded MCI, the top competitor to AT&T; Airfone and In-Flight Phone, the industry leaders in air-to-ground telephone communications; and FTD Mercury Network, the world's largest on-line floral company, handling over 25 million orders each year (IES, 1992). Could just anyone have recognized these opportunities? Did Mr. Goeken recognize these because of an "alertness" trait? Was he just plain lucky? Or, did he put himself in a position to recognize these opportunities?

It is highly unlikely that Jack Goeken was born with his ideas and opportunities, rather a complex combination of factors - the environment, work experience, education, life experiences, creativity, etc. - came together to help him recognize the opportunities surrounding him. Certainly, several of the models at the beginning of the chapter include antecedents to the recognition process which would influence the number of opportunities an individual may be exposed to. These antecedents are both within the control of the entrepreneur and outside the control of the entrepreneur. In addition, uncontrollable environmental factors which precede opportunity based on the discussions of Drucker (1985), Stevenson and Gumpert (1985) and Vesper (1993) were presented in Chapter 2. Understanding these factors is critical to understanding opportunity recognition and ultimately, entrepreneurship.

To see how different individuals are exposed to different numbers and types of opportunities we can look at the effects of culture and socio-economic status. Entrepreneurship and opportunity recognition can be fostered within ethnic enclaves as a response to the lack of opportunities within the dominant culture (Reynolds, 1992), or social and economic forces may lead to different levels of opportunity recognition (Long and McMullan, 1984). For example, a white male growing up in an upper middle class family in the suburbs of a major metropolitan city is likely to have great advantages over a black female growing up in the inner city. These advantages may allow the white male child to go on to attend a highly ranked private university while the black female may not attend college (due to different quality of education and from a financial standpoint). This difference in education, combined with racial and gender discrimination, will impact job prospects and experience. These differing life experiences will influence their world views, their abilities, and their access to information and resources and it is likely that an "entrepreneurial opportunity gap" will exist between the two people in this example. This gap represents the difference between the *potential* number of entrepreneurial opportunities and types of entrepreneurial opportunities that the two individuals may recognize, not necessarily the *actual* number that they recognize.

Thus, the numbers of opportunities individuals are exposed to vary; however, the possibility of more opportunities as a result of demographic, educational, or economic advantages does not necessarily result in opportunity recognition and successful entrepreneurship. Similarly, being "disadvantaged" does not exclude one from recognizing and taking advantage of an opportunity. For example, in his combined sample of over 230 entrepreneurs, Hills (1996) reported that approximately 25 percent did not have a college degree. However, being exposed to a higher quantity of potential opportunities through education, economic status, culture, etc., increases the chance that an entrepreneurial opportunity will be recognized. It also allows a future entrepreneur to evaluate and select out opportunities. This ability to select out an opportunity from a host of opportunities is likely to increase the probability of success because the entrepreneur will be able to weigh different opportunities against each other and select the best one. (The more opportunities, the more chances for success.)

The focus of this research is on the role entrepreneurs' social networks play on the opportunity recognition process. It is an area of research that has only been scratched on the surface, but it holds great promise because it subsumes a number of the same factors that have been proposed as antecedents to opportunity recognition. The traditional vein of entrepreneurship research has focused on characteristics, psychologies, and traits of individual entrepreneurs, but results have been inconclusive. At the other extreme is the sociological view of the entrepreneur as being a social being whose behavior and actions are guided by his/her environment and contextual factors. The study of social networks allows researchers to combine the two approaches and include both individual and environmental factors. An individual's social network is a reflection of many factors such as personality, education, socio-economic status, and geographical location. By studying a person's social network, a researcher can better understand whether the person is outgoing, friendly, part of a large family, wealthy, etc. The social circle one travels in is a good indicator of they type of person he/she is. And because social networks are a reflection of many of the same factors that have been found and/or proposed to be antecedents to opportunity recognition, there are important predictive relationships between social networks and opportunities.

The characteristics and makeup of an entrepreneur's social network should have an impact on his/her knowledge and information base. This can have a positive relationship on the numbers and types of opportunities to which the entrepreneur will be exposed, and ultimately on the numbers and types that he/she will recognize. This research attempts to identify and isolate social network characteristics that are important to the recognition of entrepreneurial opportunities. The following chapter develops hypotheses that predict the role social networks play within the opportunity recognition process, and that were subsequently tested in this study.

Opportunity Recognition and Social Networks

4.1 CHAPTER 4 INTRODUCTION

Entrepreneurship arises from innovation (Drucker, 1985; Schumpeter, 1934) and/or the exploitation of disequilibrium created by the unequal access to information by different market participants (Gilad et al., 1989; Kirzner, 1973; 1979). *Successful* entrepreneurs are those individuals who gain and control the resources necessary to bring an opportunity to fruition. Traditional research on entrepreneurs has examined the characteristics and demographic backgrounds of the individual entrepreneur (e.g., Brockhaus, 1980; Carland et al., 1988; McClelland, 1961). This would seem logical because entrepreneurs appear to be unique economic "movers and shakers" in society, but empirical study from what Gartner (1989) calls the "traits" perspective has not resulted in a conclusive "ideal type" entrepreneur (Low and MacMillan, 1988; Sexton and Bowman, 1984; Stuart and Abetti, 1990). More recently, researchers have looked for new directions to advance the entrepreneurship literature.

Over the last decade, entrepreneurship research has expanded to include research on social networks (e.g., Aldrich et al., 1987; Birley, 1985; Dubini and Aldrich, 1991; Hansen, 1995). As stated earlier, most people have contact with a great many other people (Boissevain, 1974; Burt, 1986; Pool and Kochen, 1978), and an individual's social network consists of all of the people that he/she knows (Barnes, 1972; Mitchell, 1969).

Entrepreneurial activity does not occur in a vacuum. Instead, it is embedded in cultural and social contexts, and within webs of human networks that are both social and economic (Reynolds, 1992). In fact, Johannisson (1990; p. 41) describes entrepreneurs' personal networks as the "most significant resource of the firm." Thus, shifting the level of analyses from the atomized individual characteristics of entrepreneurs to include the qualities of their social networks can help researchers study and explain opportunity recognition and entrepreneurship. Empirical studies have shown that entrepreneurs tend to use informal network contacts (e.g, family, friends, and business people) more than formal network contacts (e.g., bankers, accountants, and lawyers) as information sources (Birley, 1985; Smeltzer et al., 1988). Aldrich, et al. (1987) and Hansen (1995) found that size and interconnectivity of an entrepreneur's network significantly affects new firm performance. Zhao and Aram (1995) reported that entrepreneurs in higher growth technology firms had a greater range and intensity of business networking than did those in lower growth technology firms. However, there is scant empirical exploration of the impact of social networks on opportunity recognition. This is surprising given the fact that many entrepreneurship textbooks discuss the importance of *networking* to entrepreneurs (e.g., Stevenson et al., 1989; Vesper, 1996).

Larson and Starr (1993) proposed a network model of organization creation, but their model and discussion of the entrepreneurship process began after the opportunity had been recognized, at the stage where resources were required to create the firm. This study begins earlier in the process and examines how networks impact opportunity recognition. Early stage entrepreneurial activity involves high levels of uncertainty, but information is a valuable resource that can be used to reduce uncertainty. Stinchcombe (1990; p. 7) noted that, "what is precarious at one time becomes predictable at another time because of new information." However, no economic actor has perfect information with which to make rational choices and decisions; individuals are limited in their ability to process and store information which results in *bounded rationality* (Simon, 1976). An entrepreneur's social network ties can expand the boundaries of rationality by creating and allowing access to knowledge/information. As the boundary is extended, more new venture ideas and opportunities and potential competitive advantages may be recognized, screened and assessed, and then, if appropriate, acted upon. The personal social networks of entrepreneurs may therefore be critical to the entrepreneurial process (Dubini and Aldrich, 1991).

Access to information is not uniform across all individuals. Brittain and Freeman (1980) suggest that only people at key informational loci within social networks may be able to recognize and take advantage of opportunities. From this perspective, social networks are the key to identifying opportunities. As an example, Steve Jobs, then the cofounder and president of a newly emerging Apple Computers, was invited by business contacts at Xerox to tour the firm's research and development facilities. During the tour, he learned of graphical user interface (GUI) technology. Jobs was impressed and quietly asked for the technical details. Xerox executives who had no idea of the potential of their technology passed it on to Jobs. The GUI technology became the driving force behind the popular Apple MacIntosh operating system. Xerox could have captured a major share of the computer market, but they did not recognize the opportunity. Jobs, on the other hand, was able to recognize the opportunity, but without the business contacts at Xerox, the MacIntosh computer may never have been born.

Opportunities arise out of controllable and uncontrollable factors, and social networks are also found at the controllable/uncontrollable interface (see Figure 5). The composition of one's social network is influenced by two key elements: the individual and the environment. From a personal characteristics standpoint, an outgoing, friendly person who does not discriminate with respect to race or gender is more likely to have a large and diverse group of contacts in his/her social network than an introverted sexist and/or racist individual. In addition, the environment will impact the types of people who make up the social network. For example, a white middle-class suburban family will interact with other white middle-class suburban families, while those who live and work in ethnic minority enclaves are more likely to associate with others in their racial group.

Although the opportunity recognition process is complex, conducting social network analyses offers a promising new direction for entrepreneurship research. As discussed earlier, social network characteristics parallel a number of the same antecedents

**Figure 5. Social networks: The result of the individual/
environment interface.**

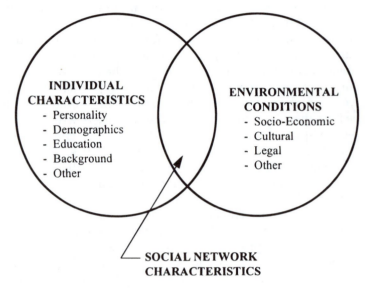

SOCIAL NETWORK
CHARACTERISTICS

that lead to opportunity recognition; they are indicators of one's
environmental context *and* individuality. Studying entrepreneurs'
social networks can be helpful to theory development and may
lead to parsimonious predictive models of opportunity recognition. Researchers can use characteristics of social networks to
represent both individual and environmental factors which can
reduce the number of variables used in analyses. However, it
should be noted that the use of social networks to recognize opportunities does not preclude the need for such variables as prior
experience or alertness. Social networks can be heavily influenced
by these variables, and thus may mediate the relationship between
them and opportunity recognition. An entrepreneur with prior
experience is likely to have business contacts within his/her network that may be important to opportunity recognition, and as
Kirzner (1979) points out, being alert to how other people's skills,
knowledge, and abilities can be utilized in a new venture will still
be beneficial to recognizing opportunities.

The entrepreneurship literature abounds with articles about
the "lone wolf," individualist entrepreneur venturing into the

unknown with little more than high hopes and a good idea. But the "network entrepreneur" is not as well understood. Does the social network impact opportunity recognition, and if so, what are its important characteristics? Are there differences, as some authors have suggested, between strong ties and weak ties (Granovetter, 1973) in an entrepreneur's network? Are structural holes (Burt, 1992) important? Do opportunity recognition and networking interact to contribute to firm performance? These are just some of the issues that need to be addressed. Further study may reveal that there are certain *types* of ties and network structures that reflect an entrepreneur's ability to recognize opportunities and competitive advantages. However, the focus herein is on what types of ties and network characteristics are important and why. To address this gap, this chapter develops and presents eighteen research hypotheses, based on social network theory and the entrepreneurship literature.

4.2 DIRECT RELEVANT RELATED LITERATURE

The Koller (1988) and Hills et al. (1997) studies (above) address the issue of opportunity recognition through social networks. Approximately half of the entrepreneurs in Koller's (1988) study recognized opportunities individually while the others recognized the opportunity through social contacts. Hills et al. (1997) found a similar proportion of solo versus network entrepreneurs and further examined the differences between the two types. They reported significant differences between solo and network entrepreneurs on a number of factors (although the measure between solo entrepreneurs and network entrepreneurs was based on a single questionnaire item). The authors called for further testing and the use of multi-item measures.

The first six hypotheses in this study seek to test the exploratory findings of Hills, et al. (1997). The fundamental hypothesis of their prior work - which was supported - was that network entrepreneurs recognized more opportunities than solo entrepreneurs. However, as discussed in Chapter 3 and indicated in Figure 4, before opportunities are recognized new venture ideas must be identified. Thus, network entrepreneurs, who have access to more information than solo entrepreneurs, are hypothesized to identify more ideas *and* more opportunities.

Hills, et al. (1997) also found that network entrepreneurs *pursued* more opportunities than solo entrepreneurs. They reasoned that this was due to having access to more information and thus, more potential opportunities. With more opportunities to select from, a network entrepreneur may recognize more attractive opportunities which they can pursue. This discussion is the basis for the first three hypotheses:

Hypothesis 1a: The greater the number of social network contacts an entrepreneur uses as idea identification sources, the greater the number of new venture ideas the entrepreneur will identify.

Hypothesis 1b: The greater the number of social network contacts an entrepreneur uses as opportunity recognition sources, the greater the number of new venture opportunities the entrepreneur will recognize.

Hypothesis 2:   The greater the number of social network contacts an entrepreneur uses as opportunity recognition sources, the greater the number of new venture opportunities the entrepreneur will pursue.

All things being equal, having a larger network will result in an entrepreneur having more information with which to identify new venture ideas and opportunities. Thus, from a social network perspective, it is likely that there are differences between solo and network entrepreneurs with respect to the range of opportunities recognized, "alertness" to opportunities, and personal experience levels in the industries of the recognized opportunities prior to firm founding.

Hills et al. (1997) found that network entrepreneurs were significantly less likely to believe that alertness and personal experience in an industry were important to opportunity recognition. They postulated that since network entrepreneurs have a larger information base (their personal knowledge plus the knowledge of others) than solo entrepreneurs, they did not have to be as sensitive or alert to recognize opportunities. In addition, network entrepreneurs did not need personal experience because social network contacts could fill in the "information gaps." However, the researchers did not find differences in the range of opportunities recognized. Theoretically, network entrepreneurs should be more likely to recognize opportunities which are unrelated to each other than solo entrepreneurs. This discussion yields the next three research hypotheses:

Hypothesis 3: The greater the number of social network contacts an entrepreneur uses as opportunity recognition sources, the wider the range of new venture opportunities the entrepreneur will recognize.

Hypothesis 4: Entrepreneurs who utilize social network contacts to recognize the new venture opportunities for their businesses will have less personal experience in the industry than those entrepreneurs who recognize new venture opportunities individually.

Hypothesis 5: Entrepreneurs who recognize new venture opportunities through their social network contacts will perceive themselves as less sensitive or alert to opportunities than those entrepreneurs who recognize opportunities individually.

Expanding on these six hypotheses, the quantity and nature of an entrepreneur's social network ties could be major sources of ideas and information (Burt, 1992; Granovetter, 1973; Hills et al., 1997). At present, research has not been conducted which clarifies how specific characteristics of social networks may be important to the opportunity recognition process. The following section develops more specific hypotheses and discusses the theoretical advantages and disadvantages of various structural characteristics of entrepreneurs' social networks to opportunity recognition.

4.3 WEAK TIES

There is an upper bound on the number of close contacts one may physically interact with because of the maintenance costs associated with more intimate relationships. However, it is possible for individuals to have many casual contacts, or weak ties, within their social network. A college acquaintance, someone met at a dinner party, members of a country club or gym, church members, or parents of a child's teammate on a little league baseball team do not require high maintenance, but can help an entrepreneur access information. This information, in turn, may lead to an entrepreneurial opportunity which may then lead to a new venture or improve upon an existing venture.

In his classic paper on the strength of weak ties, Granovetter (1973) argues that weak ties act as "bridges" to information sources not necessarily contained within an entrepreneur's immediate (strong-tie) network. In fact, Granovetter (1973) points out that because an individual does not interact with weak ties regularly, it is likely that weak ties provide more unique information than strong ties. Thus, access to weak tie sources of information may be critical for opportunity recognition by some entrepreneurs. A potential entrepreneur ("ego") who only interacts with a small group of tight-knit friends ("alters") has less chance of learning valuable information that can lead to an entrepreneurial opportunity than an ego with an extensive network of alters that includes many weak ties. Based on this argument, it is likely that entrepreneurs with an extensive number of weak ties are more likely to learn information that can lead to both new venture ideas and new venture opportunities. More formally:

Hypothesis 6a: The number of new venture ideas identified by entrepreneurs will be positively related to the number of weak ties in their social networks.

Hypothesis 6b: The number of new venture opportunities recognized by entrepreneurs will be positively related to the number of weak ties in their social networks.

4.4 STRONG AND WEAK TIES COMBINED

Strong relationships usually develop between people who have a lot of interaction between them; examples include family members, close friends, and friendly co-workers. In his 1982 review of the strength of weak ties argument, Granovetter pointed out that while weak ties provide access to unique information and resources, strong ties "have greater motivation to be of assistance and are typically more easily available" (p. 113). Close contacts, friends, and family members have ways of interacting, patterned roles, and patterned exchange relationships which overtly or covertly regulate interactions among exchange partners. Because of this fact, individuals are more likely to trust their strong-tie social contacts. In a strong-tie relationship there is an emotional bond between the parties; they are more willing to offer advice and provide information. In such a relationship, a strong-tie alter would go out of his/her way to give useful information to ego. Unlike a weak tie, a strong tie may save information about a good entrepreneurial opportunity because they are close and may want to share good fortune with a friend rather than a weak tie or stranger.

Theoretically, if an entrepreneur has many strong ties to business contacts in a variety of industries, he/she will be able to learn about many high-quality opportunities, but maintaining strong-tie relationships requires considerable time. Even if an entrepreneur could expend the improbable amount of time required to maintain strong ties to relevant business contacts in many industries, that might limit the quality of information received. In a study of clothing stores, Uzzi (1996) found that there is an inverted-U relationship between a firm's success rate and its level of embeddedness (percentage of strong ties). He looked at the structural embeddedness of each store in his sample and assessed the importance of "embedded" (strong) versus "arms-length" (weak) networks on success. Firms organized in strong, embedded networks were found to have a better chance of survival than those that did not have a network, or those that maintained weak relationships with other firms. But there was a threshold to the positive effects of embeddedness. Once the threshold was passed, there was a negative effect on the firm's chances for success. Uzzi (1996) argued that the negative effect of embeddedness may be because the network may result in "sealing-off firms in the network from new and novel information or opportunities that exist outside the network" (p. 675).

If an entrepreneur deals with one or only a few strong ties, his/her firm may become overly reliant on that (those) tie(s) for information. However, weak ties in an entrepreneur's social network may provide unique information which can provide new financial opportunities. Based on the discussion above, it appears that entrepreneurs are best served by utilizing both strong and weak ties to identify opportunities. While both strong and weak ties are important and can offer relevant information or provide valuable resources to a new venture, each type of tie can also offer different benefits. Strong ties can provide more personal information which can be trusted and reduce the need to do follow up research. Weak ties, on the other hand, can be greater in number and can thus offer more opportunities. They also provide more unique information and protect the entrepreneur from becoming too reliant on limited strong-tie sources.

Having a mix of both strong and weak ties will result in the maximum number of "good" entrepreneurial opportunities. Entrepreneurs who use both types of ties have the best of both worlds - quantity from weak ties and quality from strong ties. This "ideal mix" of ties may be different in different industries and may be affected by the individual entrepreneur's personal nature and capacity to work with other people; however, in general, an entrepreneur with a mix of strong and weak ties will greatly improve the chance of learning about opportunities worth pursuing.

> Hypothesis 7:   Entrepreneurs who utilize a mix of both strong and weak ties will recognize more successful new venture opportunities than those who utilize only strong or only weak ties, or no alters at all.

4.5 STRUCTURAL HOLES

As stated earlier, Burt's (1992) work on "structural holes" follows a rationale similar to the weak ties argument. For most people, their closest friends or relatives (strong ties) will all know each other, but casual acquaintances (weak ties) will remain anonymous to the "inner circle" of friends. Yet the casual acquaintance is more likely to provide unique information. This is due to the fact that an individual who has a group of friends who all know each other will have multiple access points to the information known by each friend - if one friend does not reveal certain information, another one may do so. Conversely, with casual relationships there is likely to be only one connection between individuals, and the loss of this connection will completely eliminate the possibility of information exchange *ever* taking place. Thus, Burt (1992) argues that it is not the actual relationship (strong or weak) between an ego and an alter, but rather the "space" between alters that predicts access to unique information. Defining the space between nonredundant contacts as "structural holes," he shows the potential benefits and importance of the holes within a network.

To clarify what structural holes are, Figure 6 contrasts a network filled with structural holes with one that is not. To understand the theory behind structural holes, let us assume an "ideal type" individual can only sustain contact with three other individuals because of the maintenance costs associated with relationships. We can see that both Entrepreneur 1 (E-1) and Entrepreneur 2 (E-2) have direct relations with only three alters, but E-1 has access to more information because of the prevalence of structural holes. (Holes separate E-1's alters and E-1 and all of the A' alters.) The benefits of structural holes should be clear, E-1 theoretically can receive information from nine alters, while E-2 is limited to only three. In addition, E-2 will be exposed to redundant information. Even if E-2 loses a direct tie with any of his/her alters, he/she will still theoretically have access to the same information, only now some information will be through indirect channels.

While a large network can offer more information, if the network is dense (everyone knows everyone else) the entrepreneur will be exposed to redundant information. Theoretically, the loss of

Figure 6. Contrasting social networks (hole-rich vs. dense).

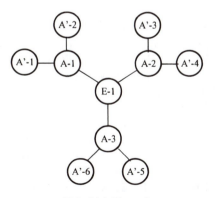

Hole-Rich Network

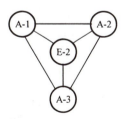

Dense Network
(No Holes)

one of the entrepreneur's alters will not significantly affect access to information. However, when an entrepreneur is connected to a network which contains many structural holes, he/she will have access to a much more expansive and diverse amount of knowledge. This can give the entrepreneur a competitive advantage in terms of recognizing and taking advantage of opportunities by exposing the entrepreneur to more nonredundant information and resources without the additional social cost of maintaining a tie to every alter within a network.

In a highly clustered network we would expect to find a close connection of nodes through reciprocated direct links in dense subsets of relations. Such an arrangement usually indicates a small network where every node is tied directly to every other node (because of the associated maintenance costs). In contrast, a hole-rich network allows for indirect and sparse chains spanning subset boundaries (Mayhew and Levinger, 1976; Wellman, 1980). This leads to the following two research hypotheses:

Hypothesis 8a: The number of new venture ideas identified by the entrepreneur will be positively related to the number of structural holes in their network.

Hypothesis 8b: The number of new venture opportunities recognized by the entrepreneur will be positively related to the number of structural holes in their network.

4.6 NETWORK DIVERSITY

"Dense" networks will limit the amount of information entrepreneurs receive partly because such networks typically contain less diverse alters (Granovetter, 1973; Campbell et al., 1986). Burt (1992) stresses that hole effects are most pronounced between actors on a social frontier. The frontier is "any place where two social worlds meet, where people of one kind meet people of a different kind" (Burt, 1992; p. 132). He goes on to point out that, "Individuals who live on a social frontier are more likely to live by their *entrepreneurial* wits than are individuals in socially homogenous environments." Thus, again using Figure 6, assuming E-1 and A-1 are different genders and different races and E-1, A-2, and A-3 are from the same gender and race, there is a greater probability of more unique information being passed between E-1 and A-1 than between E-1 and the other two alters.

A number of studies have shown that the social networks of minority and female individuals tend to be different than those of white males in terms of gender and minority heterogeneity (Ibarra, 1993; Kanter, 1977; Mehra et al., 1998; Tsui et al., 1992). Mehra et al. (1998) found that the personal social networks of minorities tend to homogenous due to both exclusionary pressures in the environment and individuals' preferences for same-race friends. However, the researchers also reported that for women, the tendency toward gender homogeneity arose primarily due to exclusionary pressures. While this study does not examine the causes for gender and racial homogeneity, it does examine the impact of having different levels of homogeneity in social networks on opportunity recognition. Based on Burt's (1992) social frontier argument and the interest in minority and female social networks, the following four hypotheses are offered:

Hypothesis 9a: Entrepreneurs who have more racially heterogeneous opportunity sources in their social network will identify more new venture ideas than those who have more racially homogeneous alters.

Hypothesis 9b: Entrepreneurs who have more racially heterogeneous opportunity sources in their social network will recognize more new venture opportunities than those who have more racially homogeneous alters.

Hypothesis 10a: Entrepreneurs who have more gender heterogeneous opportunity sources in their social network will identify more new venture ideas than those who have more gender homogeneous alters.

Hypothesis 10b: Entrepreneurs who have more gender heterogeneous opportunity sources in their social network will recognize more new venture opportunities than those who have more gender homogeneous alters.

To summarize, an entrepreneur's social network is hypothesized to be a critical source of new venture ideas and opportunities. The characteristics of one's social networks can facilitate or limit the exchange of information, which can directly lead to entrepreneurial ideas and opportunities. From the three major perspectives discussed above - weak ties, strong ties, and structural holes - it is expected that individuals with wide and diverse social networks, rich in structural holes, and intermixed with both strong and weak ties will gain information which will lead to the recognition of a greater number of new venture ideas and opportunities.

4.7 OPPORTUNITY RECOGNITION: BEFORE OR AFTER THE INTENTION TO FOUND A FIRM?

Vesper (1980) proposed that opportunities can be recognized through systematic search, and other researchers have argued that strategic planning is needed to identify opportunities (Timmons et al., 1987). However, some entrepreneurs may recognize new opportunities by chance (Teach, et al., 1989) or as part of their operations after founding a business (Ronstadt, 1988). Social encounters may be important to the recognition of these types of opportunities.

In Chapter 3, Bhave's (1994) process model of opportunity recognition was discussed in which he illustrated two processes of opportunity recognition based on Cyert and March's (1963) earlier typology: externally stimulated and internally stimulated opportunity recognition. In one there is a conscious search for the opportunity (externally stimulated), and in the other an unfilled need is identified and the opportunity emerges (internally stimulated).

Based on the discussion throughout this chapter, a network entrepreneur will be more likely to develop an internally stimulated opportunity. That is, a network entrepreneur is more likely to first recognize a need and then found a firm than is a solo entrepreneur. A chance encounter with a social contact may reveal an unfilled need which may lead to the recognition of an internally stimulated opportunity. Because network entrepreneurs have access to more information than solo entrepreneurs, they can recognize opportunities in market areas in which they have no experience. This makes it more likely that the network entrepreneur will recognize an internally stimulated opportunity.

On the other hand, a solo entrepreneur is limited to his/her personal experience and knowledge to develop an opportunity (Hills et al., 1997). Thus, solo entrepreneurs are more likely to be individuals who first make conscious decisions to start businesses and then seek to recognize opportunities. This follows the path of the externally stimulated opportunity (Bhave, 1994). Thus, it is hypothesized that there are differences in the types of opportunity recognition paths undertaken by entrepreneurs depending on their use (or non-use) of social networks. More formally:

Hypothesis 11a: An entrepreneur who first chooses to start a business and then recognizes the opportunity for the business is less likely to have used his/her social network to recognize the opportunity.

Hypothesis 11b: An entrepreneur who first recognizes the opportunity for his/her business is more likely to have used his/her social network to recognize the opportunity.

4.8 NETWORK OPPORTUNITY RECOGNITION AND FIRM PERFORMANCE

The above hypotheses predict the numbers and types of opportunities recognized through different types of social network ties. An important and logical question from a strategic management perspective is, "How does opportunity recognition through social networks affect firm performance?"

From a network perspective, researchers have debated and empirically demonstrated that size and interconnectivity of an entrepreneur's social network significantly affects new firm performance (e.g., Aldrich et al., 1987; Hansen, 1995; Nohria, 1992). These arguments have been based on the premise that networks facilitate the exchange of needed resources. However, based on the theoretical development of the hypotheses in this chapter, we should examine the performance implications of using social networks at the opportunity recognition stage.

An entrepreneur's social network can expand the boundaries of rationality (Simon, 1976) by allowing more knowledge and information to be accessed. There is some evidence that network entrepreneurs recognize more opportunities than solo entrepreneurs (Hills et al., 1997). Having more opportunities to select from should, theoretically, allow an entrepreneur to choose a better new venture option. Based on this proposition, and theoretical discussion throughout this chapter, the quality and profitability potential of an entrepreneurial opportunity could be greater if it is recognized through the entrepreneur's social network.

In addition, network entrepreneurs, by definition, are individuals who are more likely to discuss and develop their ideas with the help of outside business and social contacts. This is in contrast with solo entrepreneurs who develop the ideas for their businesses individually. While solo entrepreneurs may be more focused on the opportunity than network entrepreneurs, they may be so enamored with what they perceive to be an opportunity that they create a halo over their ideas and fail to recognize pitfalls. Solo entrepreneurs may work intensely to found the business, only to determine that the market cannot support their product or service, whereas network entrepreneurs may benefit from outside evaluation, prior to firm founding, at the opportunity recognition and development stages.

The quality of the opportunity should have an impact on business performance (see Gaglio and Taub, 1992). It is therefore proposed that network entrepreneurs will be more financially successful than solo entrepreneurs. Adding to Hypothesis 7, the final hypothesis is proposed:

Hypothesis 12:   The greater the number of social network contacts an entrepreneur uses as opportunity recognition sources, the more successful his/her firm will be.

CHAPTER 5
Research Methods

This chapter describes how the eighteen hypotheses were tested. It describes the survey questionnaire, the reasons for the chosen sample, all of the variables used in the analyses, and the statistical methods utilized.

5.1 SURVEY QUESTIONNAIRE

Data for this study were collected using a mail survey of entrepreneurs. The questionnaire was pre-tested on a convenience sample of eleven entrepreneurs. Most of the pre-test entrepreneurs who volunteered their time were affiliated with the Evanston (Illinois) Technology Park and were the founders and owners of young, emerging information technology related firms.

A full copy of the final questionnaire used in the study is attached in Appendix A. The questions include ego-network questions (Burt, 1984) to assess the personal network characteristics (i.e., homogeneity, density, strong ties, weak ties, structural holes), replicated and modified opportunity recognition measures used in prior studies (Hills, 1996; Hills et al., 1997; Koller, 1988), questions about the demographic characteristics of the sample entrepreneurs, and other questions about their businesses.

Perhaps the most interesting items in the questionnaire were the ego-network questionnaire items. These were used to assess the qualities and characteristics of social networks used by entrepreneurs to recognize opportunities (for an excellent discussion and examples of ego-network questionnaire items see Burt, 1984).

The primary benefit of an ego-network questionnaire is that it does not require a researcher to gather information about *all* of the ties within an individual's network domain, yet it provides valuable information about the structure and composition of the entrepreneur's relevant business network members. From a time and cost perspective, it is more pragmatic than a full network analysis. A prior research project (Singh et al., 1997) proved to be an invaluable learning exercise on how to use ego-network question items and helped with the specific wording of ego-network items used in this survey (e.g., Questions 17–25).

The questionnaire contained a number of replicated items used in prior published opportunity recognition research. Some of the replicated items have slight modifications from the original wording. Questions 26–27 were selected from Rotter's (1966) Internal vs. External Locus of Control Scale. Question 3 was slightly modified from a similar questionnaire item used by Koller (1988). Questions 10–16, 29, 31–33, 35–37, 39–43, and 46 were developed by Professor Gerald E. Hills at the UIC Institute for Entrepreneurial Studies. These items have been used successfully in two prior studies (Hills, 1996; Hills et al., 1997). Hills (1996) pointed out that a number of the items were replicated and modified from earlier questionnaires developed by Teach et al. (1989); Christensen and Peterson (1990); and Kaish and Gilad (1991), and that they were pretested on a convenience sample of entrepreneurs.

Personal demographic questions and other questions about entrepreneurs' current businesses were used to gather demographic information about the entrepreneurs (age, gender, race, education, etc.), firm performance, entrepreneur satisfaction with his/her firm, and other information.

A critical aspect of this study is the discussion and examination of the differences between entrepreneurial ideas and opportunities. As discussed at the end of Chapter 3, ideas lead to opportunities and the questionnaire follows the same rationale. Thus, it was important that respondent entrepreneurs understood and validated the model. Based on data collected from, and discussed with, twelve pre-test entrepreneurs, all of the entrepreneurs concurred with and understood the difference. To ensure that sample entrepreneurs understood the difference, the research model illustrated in Figure 4 in Chapter 3, a short written description of the model, and three validity check questions were included at the beginning of the questionnaire. The validity check showed strong support for the model (as discussed in Chapters 6 and 7).

5.2 THE CHOSEN SURVEY SAMPLE

For this study, a sample of entrepreneurs who were both interesting to a wide audience and important to society were selected. The sample consisted of entrepreneurs who had founded information technology (IT) consulting firms. The choice of this sample was primarily for four reasons:

1. Information technology firms are a rapidly growing segment of the economy. Journal reviewers, entrepreneurship scholars, and venture capitalists have an interest in this sample because of the rapid explosion of IT firms in recent years. Further, there is no reason to believe that the recent, rapid growth of IT firms will slow in the near future.
2. Entrepreneurs from all educational backgrounds can start such firms. Anyone can start such a firm—from computer science majors to engineering majors to business majors. Even, "computer nerds" with no formal college education often found such firms (i.e., Bill Gates dropped out of college to start Microsoft). Thus, the sample is diverse in terms of education and personal background.
3. There are a number of potential future analyses/studies that will emerge from the data (e.g., firm success for founders with computer science degrees vs. those with other degrees, differences in social networks between entrepreneurs with different personal backgrounds, comparisons to other papers that look at entrepreneurs in technology related businesses (e.g., Karagozoglu and Lindell, 1998; Teach et al., 1989)).
4. My personal interest and knowledge regarding such firms.

The IT consulting industry is a rapidly growing one that will reach $63.6 billion by the year 2000 (Zelade, 1996). It has been predicted that electronic commerce will account for six percent of the American gross domestic product in less than a decade (Hof, 1998). Because of the rapid growth of the industry, venture capital and other funding for new venture startups has dramatically increased. In 1997, more than 53,000 jobs were created in Silicon

Valley alone as venture capitalists infused a record $3.7 billion into Silicon Valley startups, which was a 60 percent increase over 1996 (Reinhardt, 1998). At the same time, there is a well-documented shortage of IT workers. The limited talent pool has created the situation where larger firms often help to fund new venture startups (Reinhardt, 1998) and often choose acquisition and merger strategies for tactical reasons to capture and combine intellectual assets (Byrne, 1998). The prevailing culture of the industry is one that promotes networking and collaboration between teaming partners (*Business Week*, 1997). All of these factors make the industry an interesting and unique industry to sample, particularly from a social network perspective.

There were two criteria which were used to narrow the firms examined: age of the firm and size of the firm. The questionnaire included retrospective items and sample entrepreneurs were required to remember how and where they recognized their opportunities, and the people they talked to about their business ideas/ opportunities prior to founding. As such, in order to minimize the error associated with memory loss, only firms that were founded within the last four years were selected.

There was a second reason for selecting young firms. During the early years of operation, many entrepreneurial ventures do not survive (Hogan, 1991; Shapero and Giglierano, 1982; Timmons, 1986; Vesper, 1996) because of the *liability of newness* (Stinchcombe, 1965). By focusing on young firms, researchers can gain insights about how successful entrepreneurship takes place during the critical early stages of a new venture.

To satisfy the second criterion, only firms with annual revenues of at least $100,000 were studied. There are many one-person firms and "mom and pop" type businesses with annual revenues under $100,000. These firms should not be trivialized, particularly when we consider the collective importance of these small firms to the economy and job creation (Birch, 1979; 1987; Kirchoff and Greene, 1995); however, firms with revenues less than $100,000 may be home-based businesses or part-time ventures and may involve different dynamics and objectives than those founded and operated as full-time ventures. By setting a revenue floor, part-time, very small, and/or no growth ventures were eliminated.

The sample of entrepreneurs for this study was obtained from Dun & Bradstreet (D&B). A total of 1,500 addresses and other information (telephone numbers, founding dates, annual revenues, number of employees, etc.) was obtained. The 1,500 entrepreneurs were from a random sample of all U.S. firms with the six-digit SIC code 7379-02 (information technology consulting) within the D&B database. The total number of possible firms in the United States with the chosen SIC code and which met the revenue and firm age requirements was approximately 26,000.

There are a number of advantages and disadvantages to using D&B as a source for identifying entrepreneurs. D&B has an extensive database of companies that can be queried on specific data fields to obtain the mailing addresses, contact (entrepreneur) names, and phone numbers for random firms across the country with specific company characteristics that satisfy the sample criteria. In addition, D&B provides performance measures such as revenues and numbers of employees, which some entrepreneurs are hesitant to provide on a mail questionnaire. These were used to compare respondents to non-respondents to test for differences between the two groups, and further to assess the representativeness of the respondent entrepreneurs (see Chapter 6).

The disadvantage of using D&B, on the other hand, is that D&B does maintain information on *all* firms in the United States (see Busenitz and Murphy, 1996). D&B information is largely used by formal lending institutions (i.e., banks and venture capital firms), investors, and government officials to review firm financial histories and backgrounds. The information is often used to determine the credit-worthiness of a firm/entrepreneur or to assess the capability of the firm to adequately finance and perform large government contracts. Researchers such as Birley (1984) and Aldrich and his associates (1989) have discussed the issues of "non-randomness" inherent with utilizing D&B data; that is, only firms that have a reason to register with D&B are in the database. Thus, firms that are founded within ethnic enclaves, or other private firms may not have any need to be a part of the D&B database.

However, the ability to identify entrepreneurs that met the study criteria and other factors outweighed the negatives. The 9,000,000 D&B companies represent approximately 98 percent of all private sector employment (D&B, 1997a; Dennis et al., 1994), and D&B is a respected source of data for a wide range of entrepreneurship studies (e.g. Chaganti and Parasuraman, 1996; Hills, 1996; Merz et al., 1994; Shane, 1996).

To summarize, U.S. entrepreneurs who had founded new information technology consulting firms, been in business for up to four years, and earned at least $100,000 in annual revenue were sampled. These firms are likely to be healthy businesses and by studying these firms we can examine the desirable characteristics of surviving firms during their early years.

5.3 SURVEY PROCEDURE

Subject entrepreneurs for this study were individuals identified as the president and/or CEO of each firm in the D&B sample. These individuals were mailed a cover letter describing the study along with a questionnaire and a self-addressed, postage-paid return envelope in November 1997. An incentive offered was a management report summarizing the results of the study. Five weeks after the initial mailing, a postcard reminder was mailed. Then a second mailing of questionnaires with cover letters was sent to nonrespondents five weeks after the postcard reminder. The first mailing was sent as bulk mail and the second was sent first class. The first class mailing was an effort to verify that all sample entrepreneur addresses were complete and deliverable because the U.S. Post Office does not return bulk mail to the sender. Copies of the two cover letters for the first and second mailings, and the wording for the postcard reminder are attached in Appendix B.

Since this study involved human subjects, the protocols for this study were submitted for approval by the Institutional Review Board (IRB) at the University of Illinois at Chicago. The research protocol met the required standards for human subject research. The specific protocols and approval from the UIC Director of the Office for Protection from Research Risks can be obtained from the author.

5.4 VARIABLES USED IN THE STATISTICAL ANALYSES

The following is a list of all variables used in the statistical analyses.

AGE - This variable was the age of the entrepreneur in years. It was taken directly from the questionnaire (Question 51).

GENDER - This was a dummy variable representing the gender of the entrepreneur. It was taken directly from the questionnaire (Question 50). The variable was coded "0" for male and "1" for female.

EDUCATION - This was the highest education level attained by the entrepreneur. It was taken directly from the questionnaire (Question 54). The values were based on an interval scale of education level, from 1=Some High School to 6=Graduate Degree.

BUSINESS DEGREE - This was a dummy coded variable for those entrepreneurs who had earned a business degree. This was based on Question 54a. Entrepreneurs who majored in business were coded as "1." All other college majors and non-college degree holding entrepreneurs were coded as "0."

ENGINEERING DEGREE - This was a dummy coded variable for those entrepreneurs who had earned an engineering degree. This was based on Question 54a. Entrepreneurs who majored in engineering were coded as "1." All other college majors and non-college degree holding entrepreneurs were coded as "0."

LIBERAL ARTS DEGREE - This was a dummy coded variable for those entrepreneurs who had earned a liberal arts degree. This was based on Question 54a. Entrepreneurs who majored in liberal arts were coded as "1." All other college majors and non-college degree holding entrepreneurs were coded as "0."

IMMIGRANT? - This was a dummy coded variable of whether the entrepreneur was an immigrant or not. This item is based on Question 53. Entrepreneurs who had immigrated to the United States were coded as "1." Those who were not immigrants were coded as "0."

WHITE RACE - This was a dummy coded variable that identified all White entrepreneurs. The measure was taken from Question 52. All White American entrepreneurs were coded as "1." All other entrepreneurs were coded as a "0."

ASIAN RACE - This was a dummy coded variable that identified all Asian entrepreneurs. The measure was taken from Question 52. All Asian American (non Indian) and Indian American (not Native American) entrepreneurs were coded as "1." All other entrepreneurs were coded as a "0."

OTHER RACE - This was a dummy coded variable to identify all non-Asian and non-White entrepreneurs. The measure is taken from Question 52. All Latino American, African American, Native American, and Other Race entrepreneurs (not White entrepreneurs) were coded as "1." All other entrepreneurs are coded as a "0." The reason for grouping all of the various ethnicities was that there were less than 10 respondents within each of the individual ethnic groups in this variable.

PRIOR EXPERIENCE - This was the number of years of experience in the industry prior to firm founding for the entrepreneurs. It was measured directly on the questionnaire (Question 45a).

OPPORTUNITY FIRST VS. INTENTION TO FOUND A FIRM FIRST - This variable was used to describe how the entrepreneur founded the firm. The determination was based on the response to Question 3. This variable was coded "1" if the entrepreneur first decided to start a firm and then searched for an opportunity for his/her business, or "2" if the entrepreneur first recognized the opportunity for the business and then founded his/her firm.

FIRM AGE - This variable was the number of years the firm had been in operation. It was calculated by subtracting the year the firm began operations (from D&B data) from 1998. This variable ranged from 1 to 4 years.

FIRM REVENUES - This variable was the firm revenues from the most fiscal year ended based on financial information provided by D&B. The log of annual revenues was used in the regression analyses in order to linearize the relationships between the independent and dependent variables (Cohen and Cohen, 1975).

NUMBER OF EMPLOYEES - This variable represented the number of employees within the firm. The number of employees was obtained from the D&B data. The log of the number of employees was used in the regression analyses in order to linearize the relationships between the independent and dependent variables (Cohen and Cohen, 1975).

SOLO VS. NETWORK ENTREPRENEURS - This was a dummy variable that distinguished those individuals who used at least one alter in their social network to recognize opportunities from those who used no one. Using Hills et al.'s (1997) nomenclature, this variable distinguishes Solo Entrepreneurs (SEs) from Network Entrepreneurs (NEs). Entrepreneurs are coded as a "1" if they are an NE or a "0" if they are an SE. The determination was based on the entrepreneur's response to Question 17. If the entrepreneur identified any alters in Question 17, they were considered an NE.

ALERTNESS TO OPPORTUNITIES - The variable was calculated by summing the responses for Questions 29, 31, and 40:

29. *While going about routine day-to-day activities, I see potential new venture ideas all around me.*

31. *I have a special "alertness" or sensitivity toward new venture opportunities.*

40. *"Seeing" potential new venture opportunities does not come very naturally to me.*

All of the items were measured on a five point Likert-scale where 5=strongly agree, 4=agree, 3=neutral, 2=disagree, and 1=strongly disagree. Question 40 was reverse coded and then added into the measure. Thus, the variable ranged from 3 to 15. The three-item scale item had an alpha of .78.

TOTAL NUMBER OF ALTERS IDENTIFIED - This variable was calculated from Questions 17 and 18. The alters listed in Question 17 and the alters identified in Question 18 were added together to create this measure.

NUMBER OF WEAK TIES - This was the number of weak tie alters used to recognize opportunities. This was determined from Question 22 and varied from 0 to 5. Question 22 asked the respondent to indicate how well he/she knew the identified alters. Alters who the respondent knew "somewhat" or "not very well" were identified as weak ties. Those individuals with no alters were coded as a "0" (see Burt, 1987).

NUMBER OF STRUCTURAL HOLES - This variable was the number of structural holes in the entrepreneur's network. This variable was calculated using Question 19 by taking all respondents with 2 or more alters (since there needs to be at least two alters to have a structural hole), and then counting the number of instances where the respondent indicated that alters knew another alter "Not at All." The range of values is from 0 to 10. All entrepreneurs who did not have any alters or only identified one alter were coded with 0 holes (see Burt, 1987).

INDEX OF QUALITATIVE VARIATION (IQV) FOR RACE - This was a measure of the racial heterogeneity of entrepreneurs' social networks. Using responses to Question 20, this variable was calculated using the Index of Qualitative Variation (IQV)[1, 2] (Agresti and Agresti, 1977). The IQV allows a researcher to statistically analyze numerical differences between nominal variables (e.g., Bienenstock et al., 1990; Marsden, 1987). This variable ranged from 0 (completely homogeneous, i.e., all alters are the same race) to 1 (completely heterogeneous, i.e., all alters are a different race).

IQV FOR GENDER - This was a measure of the gender heterogeneity of entrepreneurs' social networks. Using responses to Question 21, this variable was also calculated using the IQV (Agresti and Agresti, 1977), and ranged from 0 (all alters same gender) to 1 (all alters different gender).

MIX OF STRONG AND WEAK TIES - This was a measure of whether or not the entrepreneur used a mix of strong and weak ties to recognize the opportunity for their firm. The item is measured by taking all of the alters identified in Question 17 who had helped the entrepreneur recognize the opportunity for their current firm and then checking the tie strength to each alter based on Question 22. Entrepreneurs who identified both strong and weak ties as opportunity recognition sources are coded as a "1." All others (those who identified no alters, or only strong or only weak alters) were coded as a "0."

It should be noted that originally, Hypothesis 7 was going to be tested using a measure of tie-strength of all of the alters. This variable would have ranged from 0 (all weak tie alters) to 1 (all strong tie alters); however, there were only four respondents who only used weak ties, and many respondents with only strong ties. It was hypothesized that an inverted-U relationship existed between alter tie strength and firm success, but this relationship could not be tested. So a comparison was made between those who used only strong or weak ties and a mix of both strong and weak ties.

NUMBER OF NEW VENTURE IDEAS IDENTIFIED IN THE LAST YEAR - This was determined from Question 11:

11. *Last year, how many venture ideas did you have that could lead to potential new venture opportunities?*

Entrepreneurs could choose a number from 0 to 7, or they could select "8–10" or "11+." The choice of "8–10" was coded as a "9" and "11+" as a "12." The selection of "9" was obvious, and the choice of "12" for the "11+" response was a conservative estimate of the number of new venture ideas recognized. The measure ranged from 0 to 12. The square root transform of Question 11 was used in the regression analyses in order to linearize the relationships between the independent and dependent variables (Cohen and Cohen, 1975).

NUMBER OF NEW VENTURE OPPORTUNITIES RECOGNIZED IN THE LAST YEAR - This was determined from Question 13:

13. *Based on the ideas you had last year, how many potential new venture opportunities did you recognize?*

Entrepreneurs could choose a number from 0 to 7, or they could select "8–10" or "11+." The choice of "8–10" was coded as a "9" and "11+" as a "12." The measure ranged from 0 to 12. The square root transform of Question 13 was used in the regression analyses in order to linearize the relationships between the independent and dependent variables (Cohen and Cohen, 1975).

NUMBER OF NEW VENTURE OPPORTUNITIES UNRELATED TO CURRENT FIRM - This was measured directly from Question 14:

14. *How many of the opportunities you recognized in the last year were unrelated to your current business?*

Entrepreneurs could choose a number from 0 to 7, or they could select "8–10" or "11+." The choice of "8–10" was coded as a "9" and "11+" as a "12." The measure ranged from 0 to 12. The square root transform of Question 14 was used in the regression analyses in order to linearize the relationships between the independent and dependent variables (Cohen and Cohen, 1975).

NUMBER OF NEW VENTURE OPPORTUNITIES PURSUED IN THE LAST YEAR - This was measured directly from Question 15:

15. *In the last year, how many new venture opportunities did you pursue (invested time and money)?*

Entrepreneurs could choose a number from 0 to 7, or they could select "8–10" or "11+." The choice of "8–10" was coded as a "9" and "11+" as a "12." The measure ranged from 0 to 12. The square root transform of Question 15 was used in the regression analyses in order to linearize the relationships between the independent and dependent variables (Cohen and Cohen, 1975).

PEOPLE WHO THE ENTREPRENEUR DISCUSSED THE OPPORTUNITY WITH PRIOR TO FOUNDING - This variable was directly measured on Question 8:

8. *How many people did you discuss your potential venture opportunity with prior to founding your current firm?*

___ 0 ___ 1–2 ___ 3–4 ___ 5–6 ___ 7–8 ___9–10 ___ 11+

. Responses were coded 0, 1.5, 3.5, 5.5, 7.5, 9.5, or 12.

5.5 STATISTICAL METHODS USED TO TEST HYPOTHESES

Using the data collected, statistical methods utilizing primarily multivariate hierarchical linear regression were used to test the theoretical hypotheses. Chi-square and *t*-tests were also used in supplementary tests of several hypotheses.

Most of the hypotheses relate to how characteristics of entrepreneurs' social networks affect different dependent variables. The regression methods attempted to isolate the importance of networks and network characteristics to a variety of dependent variables. As such, the use of hierarchical regression analyses allowed for such analyses by testing the effects of the independent variables of interest after controlling for a variety of factors. For most of the regression analyses eleven control variables were entered followed by the independent variables. The control variables were:

1. Entrepreneur's age
2. Firm age
3. Immigrant
4. Education
5. Business degree
6. Engineering degree
7. Liberal arts degree
8. Asian race
9. Other race
10. Gender
11. Years of industry experience prior to firm founding

The control variables were chosen because they represented personal characteristics of entrepreneurs and their firms that could impact the dependent variables. For example, having many years of experience within an industry may lead one to recognize more opportunities because he/she is more familiar with an industry (Ronstadt, 1988).

For most of the regression analyses, the dependent variables were transformed using a log or square root function in order to linearize the relationships between the independent and dependent variables, and to achieve a normal distribution of the residuals (Agresti and Finlay, 1986; Cohen and Cohen, 1975; Norusis, 1991). The specific transforms used on variables was chosen after reviewing the frequency histogram of the regression standardized residuals. The log and square root transform was then plotted. The transform which best normalized the regression standardized residuals was then chosen as the transform function.

As described earlier in the chapter, an ego-network study is an efficient, yet less time-consuming way to analyze an individual's social network than most forms of network analysis. To test the importance of an entrepreneur's social network to opportunity recognition, a researcher would conduct extensive interviews or observe entrepreneurs over time to learn about the entire compositions of their networks. The researcher would solicit information about every person in the entrepreneur's social network and whether these network contacts were strong or weak ties. Demographic information about each alter (age, race, gender, education, etc.) would then need to be gathered, and finally, the researcher would have to find out how well each alter knew every other alter (to learn about structural holes). The importance of the overall size of the network and the numbers of strong ties, weak ties, structural holes, and other factors to opportunity recognition could then be accurately tested without bias. While this would be ideal, it is very difficult because of the time and cost required to study a large sample of entrepreneurs, as well as respondent refusals to participate. However, the ego-network study method provides a reasonable representation of an individual's overall network (Burt, 1984; 1985; Marsden, 1987; 1990; Wellman, 1993). The limitation is that the researcher cannot get a *complete* picture of an individual's network structure and composition (Wasserman and Faust, 1994).

In order to focus on salient alters for this study, entrepreneurs were asked to only provide information about people in their social network who had helped them recognize opportunities. Then, Burt's (1984) procedure for gathering specific information about five alters in the social network was utilized. This information only provides the types of alters an entrepreneur uses to help recognize opportunities. In addition, it should be noted that when using this method, there often tends to be a bias toward strong tie alters (Burt, 1986; Huang and Tausig, 1990; Marsden, 1987). This is because it is easier for respondents to remember the names and roles of strong tie alters than weak ties.

The use of ego-network question items made it possible to gather information about a large number of entrepreneurs' social networks using a mail survey. It also allowed an analysis to be conducted to study the effects of social network characteristics on opportunity recognition for entrepreneurs throughout the U.S.

NOTES

1. The Index of Qualitative Variation is calculated by using the following formula:

$$I = [k/(k-1)](1 - \sum_{i=1}^{k} p_i^2)$$

Where: k = number of categories
         p_i = sample proportions of observations in each category

For a more complete discussion see Agresti and Agresti (1978), Bienenstock et al. (1990), and Marsden (1987)

2. It should be noted that the Index of Qualitative Variation (IQV), which is used to calculate racial and gender heterogeneities, does not take into consideration differences between ego and alters, but rather only among alters. Thus, for example, a white male might only have alters who are all black females and yet receive a low score on the IQV as a measure of heterogeneity. Marsden (1987: 124) points out that the IQV "is sensitive to the diversity of alters, not to the differences between respondent and alters. For instance, a respondent might have a network composed of very similar alters, all of whom are quite different from her or him." Nonetheless, as Marsden (1987: 124) goes on to conclude: "The general tendency toward homophily in networks . . . makes the latter situation unlikely."

CHAPTER 6

Summary of Respondents and Study Sample

This chapter compares characteristics of the respondents to non-respondents and provides demographic information about the resulting sample. In addition, this chapter discusses the results of the three validity check questions at the beginning of the mail questionnaire. Finally, it provides a demographic profile of the entrepreneurs in this study.

6.1 RESPONDENT AND NONRESPONDENT CHARACTERISTICS: A COMPARISON

The sampling frame for the study was obtained from Dun and Bradstreet (D&B). Of the 1,500 entrepreneurs provided by D&B, 98 (6.5 percent) were eliminated because either (1) the mailing address provided by D&B was not complete, or (2) the questionnaire was returned as undeliverable because the business had either moved without a forwarding address or had gone out of business. Of the remaining 1,402 entrepreneurs, following the two mailings and postcard reminder, a total of 308 surveys were returned for a response rate of 22 percent. This response rate is consistent with other recent published papers in the entrepreneurship literature which utilized mail surveys to collect data: Chaganti and Parasuraman, 1996 [12.3%]; Chandler and Hanks, 1994 [19%]; Fabowale et al., 1995 [18.4%]; Hills, et al., 1997 [15%]; Karagozoglu and Lindell, 1998 [23%]; Masten et al., 1995 [30%].

The Chaganti and Parasuraman (1996) and Hills, et al. (1997) papers also utilized D&B as the source for their samples.

An "entrepreneur" is defined as someone who recognizes an opportunity and creates a new venture to pursue it. This broad definition is similar to that proposed by Bygrave and Hofer (1991) and Christensen et al. (1989). Of the 308 questionnaire respondents, three franchisees were deleted and also two respondents who did not indicate that they were founders. Franchising is a form of hybrid organization (Williamson, 1979) and franchisees are often referred to as subordinates to franchisors (Ozanne and Hunt, 1971). Franchisees often face conflicts with franchisors (Phan et al., 1996) and, because of their relationships with franchisors, face different problems and organizational issues than independent new venture startups. Since the independence, risks, and actions taken by those who create independent new ventures often differs from franchisees, the three franchisees were removed from further study. This left 303 respondent entrepreneurs.

To determine if there was a difference between the entrepreneurs who completed and returned the questionnaire and those who did not, *t*-test comparisons of respondents to nonrespondents were made using data provided by D&B. These comparisons revealed that there were no significant differences between the two groups in terms of annual revenues, number of employees, or firm age. In fact, respondents and nonrespondents were nearly identical (see Table 1. Thus, it would appear that the responding group was not biased based on firm size or age.

6.2 DEMOGRAPHIC CHARACTERISTICS OF RESPONDENTS

Respondents represented 41 states and the District of Columbia. Because Silicon Valley is a major center for information technology

Table 1. Comparison of Respondents to Nonrespondents of Mail Questionnaire

Group	Average Annual Revenues	Average No. of Employees	Firm Age (Years)
Respondents	$1,141,195	11.4	2.89
Nonrespondents	$1,132,713	12.4	2.88

(IT) firms, it is not surprising that the IT consulting entrepreneurs from California for this questionnaire made up the largest group from any single state (see Figure 7). Yet, over 86 percent still came from other states. Among the other states with notable concentrations of IT entrepreneurs were Pennsylvania (7.3 percent), Texas (6.3 percent), Virginia (5.6 percent), and Illinois (5.3 percent). Two of the surveys were returned without identification codes (the respondents had apparently removed them); therefore the state and other demographic information could not be ascertained for these two firms. The responses from these two entrepreneurs were, however, retained in the dataset.

Table 2 summarizes specific demographic characteristics of the respondents. The respondents were mostly white males (82.5 percent) between the ages of 30 and 45 (60.7 percent). Most had a college degree (78.5 percent), although over 20 percent did not have a college degree. Approximately 14 percent had immigrated to the United States. The average respondent had just over 10 years experience working in the industry prior to starting their firm. It is interesting to note that almost half of the entrepreneurs had founded other firms prior to starting their current firm, and about 10 percent had founded 4 or more. Most firms earned under $400,000 in annual revenue (62.5 percent) and 55.5 percent reported having 3 or fewer employees working for the firms (including the entrepreneur).

6.3 VALIDITY CHECK QUESTIONS

Entrepreneurs within the sample were asked to respond to three validity check questions to verify whether they understood and agreed with the research model of opportunity recognition. The questions and responses are summarized in Table 3. It was clear that the responding entrepreneurs both understood the difference between ideas and opportunities and agreed with the model. This determination was critical to the overall understanding of the opportunity construct, as well as to the validity of the questionnaire responses.

As shown in Table 3 above, after reviewing the model and the verbal description of the model, 96 percent of respondents answered the first question on "idea" consistent with the model and 95 percent answered the second question consistently. Strong

Figure 7. Geographic distribution of all respondents.

NOTES: 1) 301 firms total
2) 2 firms unknown

Table 2. Demographic Summary of All Respondents to Mail Questionnaire

Demographic Characteristic	Statistical Summary	
Age of Entrepreneur	2.6% - younger than 25 years	Mean = 39.0 years
		SD = 8.5
	13.6% - 25–30 years	
	20.4% - 31–35 years	
	25.4% - 36–40 years	
	14.9% - 41–45 years	
	11.2% - 46–50 years	
	11.9% - 51 years or older	
Highest Level of EducationAchieved by the Entrepreneur	0.7% - Some High School	
	1.3% - High School Diploma	
	19.5% - Some College	
	32.7% - Bachelor's Degree	
	16.2% - Some Graduate Education	
	29.7% - Graduate Degree	
Race of Entrepreneur	2.7% - Hispanic	
	3.0% - African American	
	82.5% - White	
	3.0% - Asian American (not Indian)	
	7.0% - Indian (not Native American)	
	0.7% - Native American	
	0.7% - Other	
Gender of Entrepreneur	85.8% - Male	
	14.2% - Female	
Did the Entrepreneur Immigrate to U.S.	13.9% - Yes	
	86.1% - No	
Total Number of Businesses Founded by Entrepreneur (including Current Business)	52.6% - 1 business	
	24.2% - 2 businesses	
	12.9% - 3 businesses	
	10.2% - 4 or more businesses	

Table 2. (Continued)

Demographic Characteristic		Statistical Summary
IT Industry Experience Prior to Starting Current Firm	7.6% - No experience 18.1% - 1–3 years experience 11.6% - 4–6 years experience 29.4% - 7–10 years experience 11.1% - 11–15 years experience 11.1% - 16–20 years experience 11.1% - 21 or more years	Mean = 10.1 years SD = 7.8
Year Current Firm was Founded	7.6% - 1997 25.7% - 1996 37.3% - 1995 29.4% - 1994	
Number of Other Cofounders	42.9% - none 34.0% - 1 cofounder 14.9% - 2 cofounders 5.9% - 3 cofounders 2.3% - 4 or more cofounders	
Number of Employees	4.7% - 1 employee 29.2% - 2 employees 21.6% - 3 employees 16.0% - 4–5 employees 15.7% - 6–10 employees 7.3% - 11–20 employees 2.6% - 21–30 employees	Mean = 10.1 employees SD = 66.6

Table 2. (Continued)

Demographic Characteristic	Statistical Summary	
	2.9% - 31 or more employees	
Annual Firm Revenues	41.5% - $100,000–$200,000	Mean = $1,073,940
	21.0% - $200,001–$400,000	SD = $6,759,420
	11.6% - $400,001–$600,000	
	10.6% - $600,001–$1,000,000	
	15.3% - Over $1,000,000	

support is also evident for the validity of the model with 86 percent in agreement. This demonstrates the overall validity of the model and supports the questionnaire design.

6.4 FINAL STUDY SAMPLE

Again, much of the mail questionnaire was designed such that respondents had to agree with and understand the model presented at the beginning of the questionnaire. Fewer than eight percent of the respondents did not agree with the model; however another 23 either answered that they were not sure if they agreed with the model and/or answered one of the first two questions inconsistently with the model. Therefore, of the 303 respondents, 47 were found to have answered one or more of the validity check questions inconsistently with the model. For purposes of analysis, the 47 individuals who did not agree and/or understand the model were deleted. Although *t*-test comparisons of the 256 individuals who understood and agreed with the model to the 47 who did not revealed that there were no significant differences between the two groups in terms of age, education, years of prior experi-

Table 3. Respondent Responses to Validity Check Questions

Question Wording	Results
A. When someone first thinks of a possible new venture, but has not evaluated it much at all, this survey would call it a "new venture _____."	96.0% - Idea 1.0% - Opportunity 3.0% - Not clearly either of these
B. When someone has given a possible new venture some additional thought and/or evaluation, this survey would say that it may lead to a "new venture _____."	2.0% - Idea 95.0% - Opportunity 3.0% - Not clearly either of these
C. Do you agree that the steps in the model illustrated above *generally* occur as shown?	86.1% - Yes 7.9% - No 5.9% - Not Sure

ence, annual firm revenues, or number of employees, the 47 had to be removed because it could not be ascertained whether they could distinguish between ideas and opportunities. Further analyses of respondents who did not answer the validity questions as expected are shown in the supplementary analyses discussed in Chapter 10.

The final count of entrepreneurs used in this study was 256, which represented an 18.3 percent useable response rate (84.5 percent of the mail questionnaire respondents). The frequency distributions were very similar to those shown in Table 1. The mean revenues and number of employees were $1,150,145 and 10.8, respectively. The average age was 38.7 years and the entrepreneurs had on average 9.8 years of prior experience before founding their firms. Table 4 summarizes the demographic information for the sample of entrepreneurs who were used to test the hypotheses and Figure 8 provides the geographic distribution of the study sample respondents. Based on both Table 5 and Figure 8, there appears to be no bias or difference between those entrepreneurs who agreed with the model and those who did not.

Table 4. Demographic Summary of Entrepreneurs in this Study

Demographic Characteristic	Statistical Summary	
Age of Entrepreneur	2.7% - younger than 25 years 13.7% - 25–30 years 21.1% - 31–35 years 25.8% - 36–40 years 14.8% - 41–45 years 11.4% - 46–50 years 10.5% - 51 years or older	Mean = 38.7 years SD = 8.3
Highest Level of Education Achieved by the Entrepreneur	0.4% - Some High School 0.4% - High School Diploma 19.9% - Some College 34.9% - Bachelor's Degree 16.8% - Some Graduate Education 27.7% - Graduate Degree	
Race of Entrepreneur	3.1% - Hispanic 2.4% - African American 82.7% - White 3.5% - Asian American (not Indian) 6.7% - Indian (not Native American) 0.8% - Native American 0.8% - Other	
Gender of Entrepreneur	86.3% - Male 13.7% - Female	

Table 4. (Continued)

Demographic Characteristic	Statistical Summary	
Did the Entrepreneur Immigrate to U.S.	14.5% - Yes 85.5% - No	
Total Number of Businesses Founded by Entrepreneur (including Current Business)	51.8% - 1 business 24.7% - 2 businesses 13.3% - 3 businesses 10.2% - 4 or more businesses	
IT Industry Experience Prior to Starting Current Firm	10.9% - No experience 11.8% - 1–3 years experience 17.9% - 4–6 years experience 19.2% - 7–10 years experience 18.3% - 11–15 years experience 15.7% - 16–20 years experience 6.2% - 21 or more years	Mean = 9.8 years SD = 7.6
Year Current Firm was Founded	7.0% - 1997 28.5% - 1996 34.4% - 1995 30.1% - 1994	
Number of Other Cofounders	42.6% - none 34.0% - 1 cofounder 16.0% - 2 cofounders 5.5% - 3 cofounders 2.0% - 4 or more cofounders	
Number of Alters who Helped Entrepreneur	8.6% - 0 alters 11.7% - 1–2 alters 14.1% - 3 alters	Mean = 5.8 alters SD = 6.1 Maximum = 24

Table 4. (Continued)

Demographic Characteristic	Statistical Summary	
Recognize Opportunities	10.9% - 4 alters 0.7% - 5 alters 14.9% - 6–7 alters 12.9% - 8–11 alters 6.3% - 12 or more alters	
Number of Employees	4.3% - 1 employee 29.1% - 2 employees 21.7% - 3 employees 17.3% - 4–5 employees 14.6% - 6–10 employees 7.1% - 11–20 employees 2.8% - 21–30 employees 3.1% - 31 or more employees	Mean = 10.8 employees SD = 72.5
Annual Firm Revenues	40.9% - $100,000–$200,000 22.1% - $200,001–$400,000 11.4% - $400,001–$600,000 11.0% - $600,001–$1,000,000 14.6% - Over $1,000,000	Mean = $1,150,145 SD = $7,347,181

Figure 8. Geographic distribution of study entrepreneurs.

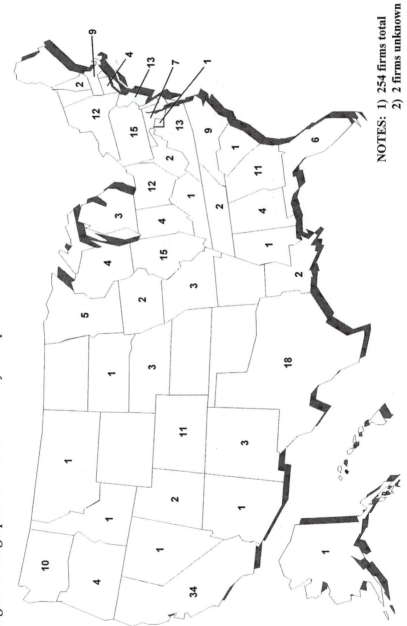

NOTES: 1) 254 firms total
2) 2 firms unknown

CHAPTER 7

Ideas vs. Opportunities: Empirical Data Results

Consistent with the research model, there were differences perceived by respondents between new venture ideas and opportunities. The findings in this chapter examine entrepreneurs' idea sources and how they develop their opportunities from their ideas.

7.1 NUMBERS OF IDEAS IDENTIFIED AND OPPORTUNITIES RECOGNIZED

Tables 5 and 6 summarize the results of respondent self reports of the numbers of new venture ideas and opportunities that they identified. Consistent with the earlier discussion of entrepreneurial opportunities, we can see that entrepreneurs identified more ideas than opportunities. Tables 5 and 6 also support the concept that not all ideas are opportunities. In fact, there were no respondents who reported more opportunities than ideas, providing further evidence that the respondents understood and confirmed the distinctions in the model.

7.2 SOURCES OF IDEAS

Entrepreneurs were asked where they obtained the initial idea for their business venture. Table 7 presents the reported idea sources.

Personal experience was by far the most important source of new venture ideas that led to the founding of firms (73 percent).

Table 5. Numbers of New Ventures Ideas Identified and Opportunities Recognized: Percentages of Entrepreneurs

ITEM	Number of Ideas Identified/Opportunities Recognized									
	0	1	2	3	4	5	6	7	8–10	11+
Ideas last month	14.6%	25.3	22.9	15.8	9.5	7.1	1.2	0.0	0.8	2.8
Ideas last year	2.4	8.3	8.7	10.7	7.1	11.9	8.7	2.4	12.3	27.7
Opportunities last month	33.2	37.9	18.6	6.7	1.6	0.8	0.0	0.4	0.0	0.8
Opportunities last year	10.7	18.2	23.7	14.2	10.7	8.3	3.2	0.8	3.2	7.1

n=253 (3 respondents did not respond to these questions)

Table 6. Mean Numbers of Ideas Identified and Opportunities Recognized

Item	Mean	St. Dev.
Ideas last month	2.4	2.3
Ideas last year	6.6	4.1
Opportunities last month	1.2	1.5
Opportunities last year	3.3	3.1

n=253 (3 respondents did not respond to these questions)

This is not surprising given that the entrepreneurs in this study had an average of almost 10 years of industry experience prior to starting their business. This evidence further confirms that many entrepreneurs found businesses based on their prior experience (Vesper, 1996).

Social network contacts were also important to idea identification. A large percentage of entrepreneurs identified business associates (32.8 percent) and friends and family (19.1 percent) as the source of the ideas for their business. Many entrepreneurs also reported that they saw a similar business (25.8 percent) which led them to their business idea.

Table 7. Where Entrepreneurs Obtain Their New Venture Ideas*

Source	Percentage of Respondents
Prior Experience	73.0%
Business Associates	32.8%
Saw a Similar Business	25.8%
Friends or Relatives	19.1%
Hobby/Personal Interest	17.2%
Market Research	11.3%
It Just Came to Mind	10.9%
Magazine/Newspaper	2.3%
Radio/Television	0.4%
Other	4.7%

n=256

* respondents could indicate as many sources as applicable

Most of the 25.8 percent of entrepreneurs who reported that they had seen a similar business also based the ideas for their firms on personal experience (66.7 percent of those who reported seeing a similar business). This would further indicate that these individuals modeled their firms on companies that they had worked in. Many of the entrepreneurs in this sample probably worked for information technology firms and realized that they could provide services themselves.

A closer analysis of the social network sources found that approximately 42 percent indicated that they identified the idea for their business from business associates, friends, or family. The percentage is consistent with the findings of two other empirical studies which looked at social network information sources for new venture ideas (Hills et al., 1997; Koller, 1988). In addition, the responses revealed that of those entrepreneurs who reported getting the idea from business associates, over 72 percent also indicated that the idea was based on prior experience. It seems reasonable to assume that working in an industry provides access to social contacts that can help an entrepreneur identify new venture ideas within that industry. (Of the entrepreneurs who indicated that friends were important idea sources, 61.2 percent also indicated prior experience was one of their idea sources.)

7.3 TURNING IDEAS INTO OPPORTUNITIES

As discussed throughout this study and as predicted both in the research model and the model of an entrepreneurial opportunity (Figure 3), entrepreneurs must take some action or conduct further evaluations to turn ideas into opportunities. Table 8 presents the activities that were performed by entrepreneurs in the sample.

Once again, Table 8 presents evidence of the importance of social networks to opportunity recognition. The results show that entrepreneurs discussed their new venture ideas with potential clients/customers (50 percent), friends and family (46.5 percent), and/or sought out information/feedback from business associates (52 percent). In fact, 75 percent of the respondent entrepreneurs marked at least one of the above social network activities as being part of their opportunity recognition process.

The respondents have experienced a certain amount of success—survival itself is no small achievement and they gener-

Table 8. Activities Conducted by Entrepreneurs Which Turned New Venture Ideas Into Opportunities*

Activity	Percentage of Respondents
Sought out information/feedback from business associates	52.0%
Contacted potential customers/clients	50.0%
Discussed idea with friends/family members	46.5%
Gathered information on competitors	33.6%
None, just knew idea was an opportunity	33.2%
Prepared financial statements	25.0%
Other	3.5%

n=256

* respondents could indicate as many sources as applicable

ate at least $100,000 in annual revenues—using social networks in the opportunity recognition process may be one way to help reduce the liability of newness (Stinchcombe, 1965). By actively engaging in exchange behaviors with relevant personal contacts (potential clients, friends, business contacts, family members), entrepreneurs may be better equipped to obtain resources such as financial backing, psychological support, physical goods, and business information to facilitate their ventures' survival (Aldrich, et al., 1987; Hansen, 1995; Hansen and Allen, 1992). This may be critical because most new enterprises lack the experience and resources needed to develop a resistance to the liability of newness, and further, to establish competitive ability through internal structural adaptation (Lawrence and Lorsch, 1967). Organizations depend on resource exchange in their environment for survival and goal achievement; however, new ventures lack the more refined abilities of acquiring resources and information processing functions necessary for growth and survival that established firms have developed (Aldrich and Herker, 1977). If an entrepreneur discusses a business idea with his/her alters and then recognizes the idea as an opportunity, he/she has gained the input and knowledge of others which may provide insight into the quality of the opportunity. It would have been useful to examine those firms that failed. If the entrepreneurs of those firms did not use their social networks, or did not use them as often, we would have additional evidence in support of the importance of social networks within entrepreneurship. Future research should look at those firms that fail to test if there is a difference in the use of social network contacts during opportunity recognition process.

A potentially interesting subgroup of entrepreneurs is the one that "just knew" the idea was an opportunity (33.2 percent). This item was intended to be an exclusive item, however, 29 of the 85 respondents who responded, "None, I knew my business idea was an opportunity" also indicated at least one other opportunity recognition activity. These respondents may have felt strongly that the new venture idea was an opportunity and also conducted some other confirmatory activity(ies) to verify their belief. Further study of this subgroup may reveal interesting differences in the type of individual personality or background of these entrepreneurs.

7.4 TIMESPAN BETWEEN INITIAL IDEA AND OPPORTUNITY RECOGNITION

Entrepreneurs were asked to identify the approximate length of time, if any, that elapsed between when they first identified the idea for their firm and when they recognized the opportunity for their business. As expected, respondents were able to distinguish the duration of time between the two events, and interestingly, there was also a wide distribution of time reported. Table 9 summarizes the results.

Table 9. Timespan Between Idea Identification and Opportunity Recognition

Time	Percentage of Entrepreneurs
None	13.7%
Hours	2.3%
Days	14.5%
Weeks	22.7%
Months	35.9%
Years	10.9%

n=256

For most entrepreneurs, a substantial amount of time passed before the idea for their business became the *opportunity* for their business. Over 45 percent of the entrepreneurs described the length of time to be months and even years. For about 37 percent of the entrepreneurs, their ideas were recognized as opportunities within a matter of days or weeks. A much smaller portion of entrepreneurs were those who recognized opportunities from their ideas in little or no time (16 percent).

While 84 percent of the respondents reported that the timespan between idea identification and opportunity recognition was days, weeks, months, and years, 16 percent took no time. It may have been that those individuals with more experience did not need to take any time to consider whether an opportunity existed— they would know because they had the personal background to understand that their idea was an opportunity. However, further analysis of those entrepreneurs revealed that they did not have significantly more prior experience than the entrepreneurs who reported longer timeframes between idea identification and opportunity recognition. In the future, more refined measures will be used to better understand the differences between these groups.

7.5 TIMESPAN BETWEEN OPPORTUNITY RECOGNITION AND FIRM FOUNDING

As proposed in the research model, after the opportunity was recognized, a period of time usually elapsed before the entrepreneur founded his/her firm. As with the timing between idea generation and opportunity recognition, 61 percent of the entrepreneurs took months or years to start their firm (see Table 10). Less than 13 percent of the entrepreneurs reported only taking hours or days, while 26.2 percent reported taking weeks. This, combined with the results in Table 9, demonstrate that most entrepreneurs take time before starting a business. This is not surprising until we consider the length of time. The fact that most entrepreneurs appear to take months and even years from the time they first realize their initial venture idea to when they start their firm begs the question of what happens in that time frame. Some researchers have studied nascent entrepreneurs (Carter et al., 1996; Reynolds, 1994; White and Reynolds, 1997) and developed stage models that describe the early entrepreneurship process (e.g., Bird, 1992; Herron and

Table 10. Timespan Between Opportunity Recognition and Actual Firm Founding

Time	Percentage of Entrepreneurs
Hours	1.6%
Days	11.3%
Weeks	26.2%
Months	50.8%
Years	10.2%

n=256

Sapienza, 1992; Learned, 1992; Van de Ven et al., 1984); however, little research has looked at opportunity recognition activities and models focus on activities that occur after opportunity recognition just prior to firm founding. More work is needed with respect to developing opportunity recognition models.

7.6 MODIFICATION OF INITIAL VENTURE IDEA BEFORE OPPORTUNITY RECOGNITION

During the time period prior to opportunity recognition, it is likely that the initial idea or conception of the business is modified as the opportunity takes shape. In order to test whether any modification took place, entrepreneurs were asked to report the amount of change that occurred with their business ideas before they were recognized as opportunities. Table 11 summarizes the results.

As can be seen in Table 11, most entrepreneurs did make some change to their initial venture idea before it became an opportunity. For many it was just a slight change (42.6 percent); however, 28.5 percent reported making a moderate change and almost ten percent made a major or complete change in their business idea. Again, the respondents had an average of ten years of experience in their industry prior to founding. This may give us some insight into why changes were minimal. But, even with an average of ten years of personal experience, over one third of the entrepreneurs made a moderate, major, or complete change to their business idea.

Table 11. Amount of Modification to Idea Prior to Opportunity Recognition

Change	Percentage of Entrepreneurs
No Change	19.1%
Slight Change	42.6%
Moderate Change	28.5%
Major Change	9.0%
Complete Change	0.8%

n=256

7.7 MODIFICATION OF INITIAL VENTURE IDEA BEFORE FIRM FOUNDING

Table 12 summarizes the amount of change to the idea that occurred between the time the initial venture idea was conceived and the firm was founded. Again, we see that for many it was just a slight change (43.9 percent); however, 28.2 percent reported making a moderate change and over five percent made a major or complete change in their business idea. As stated in the previous section, the entrepreneurs' prior experience probably accounts for the minimal changes to the new venture idea prior to firm founding. But, even with 10 years of personal experience, over one third of the entrepreneurs made a moderate, major, or complete change to their business idea.

It should be noted that results shown in Table 12 seem to indicate a misunderstanding of the questionnaire item used to measure

Table 12. Amount of Modification to the Idea Prior to Form Founding

Change	Percentage of Entrepreneurs
No Change	22.4%
Slight Change	43.9%
Moderate Change	28.2%
Major Change	5.5%
Complete Change	0.0%

n=256

the modification to the new venture idea before firm founding by some entrepreneurs. Table 11 shows the changes that took place as the idea became an opportunity and Table 12 shows the changes to the idea that occurred before firm founding. We would expect to see more change over time. However, more respondents indicated that there was no change between the idea identification and firm founding (Table 12), than between idea identification and opportunity recognition (Table 11). There may have some respondents who misread the question and thought about modifications to the "opportunity" before firm founding. On the two question items immediately preceding the question item summarized in Table 12, entrepreneurs were asked about the time between the *opportunity* and firm founding. It is reasonable to assume that some entrepreneurs read the question item quickly and made the mistake of not realizing that the questionnaire was asking for the change to the *idea*.

Opportunity recognition is a process, rather than a "eureka" event (Hills, et al., 1997). Taken together, the results shown in Tables 11 and 12 support the possibility of a feedback loop within the opportunity recognition process. Future studies of opportunity recognition should attempt to better understand the specific changes to new venture ideas that occur, and the feedback mechanisms that create the changes while keeping the opportunity recognition process moving toward firm founding.

7.8 ROLE OF SOCIAL CONTACTS IN THE OPPORTUNITY RECOGNITION PROCESS

We have seen that in both the idea generation and opportunity recognition processes, social contacts are important. As stated earlier, 75 percent of all entrepreneurs reported that they had contacted friends, family, potential clients/customers, and/or business associates as part of the opportunity recognition process. To better understand this part of the process, entrepreneurs were asked to indicate how many outside social contacts they had discussed their opportunity with prior to firm founding and how much of an influence their discussions had on modifying their opportunities. Table 13 summarizes the numbers of contacts entrepreneurs spoke with, and Table 14 provides information about the resulting amount of modification based on the discussions.

Table 13. Number of Social Contacts the Entrepreneur Discussed the Opportunity with Prior to Firm Founding

Number of Contacts	Percentage of Entrepreneurs
None	2.3%
1–2	15.6%
3–4	24.6%
5–6	28.1%
7–8	11.3%
9–10	5.5%
11 or more	12.5%

n=256

More than half the entrepreneurs indicated that they discussed their opportunities with 3–6 alters. Less than 20 percent discussed with two or fewer alters and just under 30 percent discussed with seven or more alters. In fact, only 2.3 percent reported that they did not discuss their opportunity with anyone, again providing further support for the importance of entrepreneurs' social networks to the opportunity recognition process.

Table 14 provides insight into the specific role of social networks within the opportunity recognition process. Almost 50 percent of the respondents indicated that after they had recognized the opportunity for their firm, discussions with social contacts led to slight changes in their opportunities. We can see that just over

Table 14. Modifications to Opportunity After the Opportunity was Recognized as a Result of Discussions with Social Contacts

Change	Percentage of Entrepreneurs
No Change	29.2%
Slight Change	49.2%
Moderate Change	19.2%
Major Change	2.4%
Complete Change	0.0%

n=256

29 percent of the entrepreneurs reported no change in their opportunity as a result of their discussions. Table 14 provides evidence that may indicate that social networks play a role in "fine-tuning" opportunities before business founding. Entrepreneurs may seek out the advice/opinions of others in their social network in order to verify that their perceived opportunity is indeed an opportunity. The feedback that they receive may help to refine the opportunity into a better opportunity. Thus, social networks can play a dual role - they may help an entrepreneur recognize the opportunity (see Table 8) as well as refine the opportunity.

7.9 CONCLUDING REMARKS ABOUT CHAPTER 7

Overall, the findings in this chapter support the model that proposes that ideas and opportunities are distinct constructs and that different processes take place at different times within the opportunity recognition process. The evidence also reveals that the processes of opportunity recognition and firm founding in the IT consulting industry may be long and protracted which is surprising given that IT consulting is also a rapidly growing industry (Reinhardt, 1998; Zelade, 1996). Over the next few years, as the industry continues to grow, the time between idea identification and firm founding may get shorter as more and more entrepreneurs enter the industry. It is unclear how these results might compare to other industries. Because this industry is rapidly expanding, one might expect the experience levels of founding entrepreneurs to be lower as they enter the market quickly. On the other hand, the substantial pay for workers in the industry may keep them from taking the risk of founding their own firm.

Based on the empirical results summarized in this chapter, there is strong evidence that social networks play a vital role in the pre-organization stage of an entrepreneurial venture. However, it should be noted that IT consulting entrepreneurs may be more likely to discuss opportunities with others because of the "networking" culture of the technology industry (Reinhardt, 1998). In fact, *Business Week* recently published a special double issue detailing the open culture that promotes networking and collaboration between teaming partners in Silicon Valley (*Business Week*, 1997). Empirical tests using other samples may not yield the same results, in terms of the importance of social networks to opportunity recognition.

These results point to a number of future research needs. Researchers should study other industries and all aspects of how an idea becomes an opportunity. In addition, more research is need on the pre-founding activities during what is often a substantial time period between new venture idea identification and firm founding may be useful for further understanding of the opportunity recognition process. More specifically, longitudinal study using both quantitative and qualitative data should be conducted to better understand the specific activities that occur and the relative importance of each activity.

CHAPTER 8

Empirical Results: Tests of Hypotheses

This chapter presents the results of the statistical analyses used to test the research hypotheses. Tables summarizing the results are found at the end of this chapter. Table 15 summarizes the descriptive statistics (means, standard deviations, and correlations) for all variables used in the analyses.

8.1 EXAMINING THE NUMBERS OF NEW VENTURE IDEAS IDENTIFIED

Hypotheses 1a, 6a, 8a, 9a, and 10a were tested using hierarchical regression analyses. The square root transform of the number of ideas entrepreneurs recognized in the last year was regressed on the eleven control variables (age, gender, race, education, college major, immigrant, years of prior experience, and firm age) and then on the independent variables. The square root transform was performed on the number of ideas identified in order to linearize the relationship between the independent and dependent variables and to better achieve a normal distribution of the residuals (Agresti and Finlay, 1986; Cohen and Cohen, 1975; Norusis, 1991). Table 16 summarizes statistical results for tests of the effects of various independent variables on the square root of the numbers of new venture ideas entrepreneurs identified in the last year.

It should be noted that the total number of alters variable is the total number of alters that helped the entrepreneur recognize

Table 15. Descriptive Statistics and Correlations

Variable	Mean	SD	1	2	3	4	5	6	7	8
1. Age	38.74	8.29	1.00							
2. Firm Age	2.88	.92	.05	1.00						
3. Immigrant[a]	.86	.35	.03	-.12	1.00					
4. Education	4.50	1.13	.30***	.01	-.20***	1.00				
5. Business Major[a]	.23	.42	.13*	-.01	.04	.19**	1.00			
6. Engineering/Science Major[a]	.21	.41	-.04	.01	-.11	.13*	-.28***	1.00		
7. Liberal Arts Major[a]	.11	.31	.06	-.16**	.07	.09	-.19**	-.18**	1.00	
8. Race - Asian (Indian/Oriental)[a]	.10	.30	-.13*	.13*	-.56***	.14*	-.03	.11	-.03	1.00
9. Race - Other (Black/Hispanic/Other)[a]	.07	.26	.04	-.09	-.02	.01	.03	-.07	-.10	-.09
10. Gender[a]	.14	.34	.16*	.02	.03	.05	.11	-.12*	.12*	-.02
11. Prior Experience	9.76	7.63	.54***	.07	.06	.09	-.02	.07	-.06	-.13*
12. Self-Perceived Alertness	.77	.14	-.06	.07	-.01	-.02	.02	-.08	.11	-.03
13. Total Number of Alters Identified	5.29	3.93	-.02	-.11	.14*	-.07	.00	.00	.01	-.10
14. Log # of Employees	.61	.39	.06	-.03	-.02	.08	.18**	-.10	-.04	-.01
15. Number of Structural Holes	2.66	2.76	.03	-.11	.10	-.08	-.10	-.07	.06	-.11
16. Racial Heterogeneity of Alters	.15	.27	.03	.07	-.06	.01	.11	-.07	.02	.18**
17. Gender Heterogeneity of Alters	.52	.39	.03	.03	.08	-.03	-.02	-.00	-.01	-.10

Table 15. (Continued)

Variable	Mean	SD	1	2	3	4	5	6	7	8
18. Mix of Strong and Weak Ties[a]	.20	.40	.12	-.02	-.04	-.08	-.04	-.03	.12	.09
19. Q3_How (business or opportunity first)[a]	1.88	.33	.06	-.15*	.05	.05	.03	.02	-.11	-.08
20. Q8 (# of alters who E discussed op with)	5.51	3.29	.03	-.13*	.04	-.03	.07	-.04	.01	-.18**
21. Q11_SQRT (# of Ideas last year)	2.40	.90	-.11	-.09	.15*	-.12	-.04	-.04	-.03	-.20**
22. Q13_SQRT (# of Opportunities last year)	1.60	.86	-.02	.00	.05	-.12	-.08	-.14*	.07	-.12
23. Q14 (# of unrelated opps to business)	1.21	1.97	-.02	-.01	.07	-.03	.07	-.05	.00	-.01
24. Q14_SQRT (square root of q14)	.67	.66	-.04	.01	.15	.03	.08	-.16	-.01	-.09
25. Q15 (# of Opps. Pursued last year)	1.85	2.06	-.02	.00	.12	-.05	-.08	-.05	.03	-.13
26. Q15_SQRT (square root of q15)	1.15	.73	.04	-.04	.12	-.02	-.08	-.10	.07	-.16
27. Log of Annual Firm Revenues	5.54	.46	.03	.01	-.07	.11	.25***	-.08	-.08	.02
28. Solo_Net (solo vs. network E's)[a]	.78	.41	-.06	-.08	.11	-.07	.08	-.12	-.03	-.04
29. # of Weak Ties	.52	.87	.13*	-.03	-.05	-.03	-.04	-.02	.10	.02

Table 15. (Continued)

Variable	9	10	11	12	13	14	15	16	17	18
9. Race - Other (Black/Hispanic/Other)[a]	1.00									
10. Gender[a]	-.02	1.00								
11. Prior Experience	-.02	.00	1.00							
12. Self-Perceived Alertness	-.03	.03	-.11	1.00						
13. Total Number of Alters Identified	.04	-.08	.14*	.13*	1.00					
14. Log # of Employees	.00	-.05	.03	.17**	.17**	1.00				
15. Number of Structural Holes	.03	-.02	.04	.21***	.44***	.05	1.00			
16. Racial Heterogeneity of Alters	.12	.12*	-.05	-.08	-.13*	-.09	.00	1.00		
17. Gender Heterogeneity of Alters	.15	.04	.06	.01	.18**	.06	.12	.13*	1.00	
18. Mix of Strong and Weak Ties[a]	-.06	.14	.16**	.01	.14*	.06	.23***	-.02	-.02	1.00
19. Q3_How (business or opportunity first)[a]	.01	-.06	-.05	-.04	.06	-.02	.01	-.02	-.02	-.02

Table 15. (Continued)

Variable	9	10	11	12	13	14	15	16	17	18
20. Q8 (# of alters who E discussed op with)	-.07	.00	.04	.14*	.42***	.17**	.26***	-.11	.05	.06
21. Q11_SQRT (# of Ideas last year)	-.02	-.11	-.05	.44***	.32***	.11	.23***	-.14*	.05	.04
22. Q13_SQRT (# of Opportunities last year)	-.08	-.01	.01	.36***	.23***	.07	.19**	-.02	.04	-.01
23. Q14 (# of unrelated opps to business)	.05	.04	-.12	.20**	.12	.11	.07	.05	.14*	.02
24. Q14_SQRT (square root of q14)	.05	.12	.03	.26***	.19*	.09	.21*	.01	.19*	.00
25. Q15 (# of Opps. Pursued last year)	-.08	-.03	.06	.20***	.21***	.00	.16*	-.09	.00	.06
26. Q15_SQRT (square root of q15)	-.07	.02	.05	.22***	.15*	-.05	.11	-.07	-.03	.06
27. Log of Annual Firm Revenues	-.02	-.07	-.02	.14*	.10	.90***	.00	-.01	.02	.08
28. Solo_Net (solo vs. network E's)[a]	.03	.02	.01	-.03	.34***	.11	.21***	-.07	-.02	.26***
29. # of Weak Ties	-.08	.05	.06	.07	.16**	.03	.38***	-.06	-.06	.63***

Table 15. (Continued)

Variable	19	20	21	22	23	24	25	26	27	28	29
19. Q3_How (business or opportunity first)[a]	1.00										
20. Q8 (# of alters who E discussed op with)	.06	1.00									
21. Q11_SQRT (# of Ideas last year)	.06	.25***	1.00								
22. Q13_SQRT (# of Opportunities last year)	.06	.19**	.66***	1.00							
23. Q14 (# of unrelated opps to business)	.03	.01	.34***	.33***	1.00						
24. Q14_SQRT (square root of q14)	.07	.02	.42***	.43***	.91***	1.00					

Table 15. (Continued)

Variable	19	20	21	22	23	24	25	26	27	28	29
25. Q15 (# of Opps. Pursued last year)	.02	.13*	.38***	.58***	.05	.11	1.00				
26. Q15_SQRT (square root of q15)	.04	.10	.39***	.59***	.09	.15	.91***	1.00			
27. Log of Annual Firm Revenues	-.05	.13*	.07	.07	.10	.08	-.02	-.08	1.00		
28. Solo_Net (solo vs. network E's)[a]	.04	.09	.18**	.11	.07	.22*	.13*	.14*	.11	1.00	
29. # of Weak Ties	.01	.07	.18	.17**	.03	.08	.17**	.20***	.02	.14*	1.00

$N = 256$

[a] Dummy Variable

* p < .05 ** p < .01 *** p < .001

Table 16. Results of Regression Analyses for the Square Root of the Number of New Venture Ideas Identified by Respondents in the Last Year

Variable[‡‡]	Model 1	Model 2	Model 3	Model 4
		Hyp. 1a	Hyp. 6a, 8a, 9a, 10a	BEST FIT/Hyp. 6a
	Beta	Beta	Beta	Beta
Controls				
Age	–.091	–.058	–.087	–.088
Firm Age	–.062	–.035	–.027	–.031
Immigrant	.041	.006	.023	.021
Education	–.035	–.021	–.010	–.008
Business Major	–.045	–.056	–.037	–.049
Engineering/Science Major	–.060	–.068	–.063	–.066
Liberal Arts Major	–.053	–.063	–.070	–.075
Race – Asian (Indian/Oriental)	–.178*	–.180*	–.164*	–.180*
Race – Other (Black/Hispanic/Other)	–.052	–.067	–.047	–.053
Gender	–.086	–.067	–.071	–.075
Prior Experience	–.020	–.077	–.068	–.069
Total Number of Alters Identified		.304***	.249***	.275***
Number of Weak Ties			.142*	.159**

Table 16. (Continued)

Variable[††]	Model 1	Model 2	Model 3	Model 4
		Hyp. 1a	Hyp. 6a, 8a, 9a, 10a	BEST FIT/Hyp. 6a
	Beta	Beta	Beta	Beta
Number of Structural Holes			.054	
Racial Heterogeneity of Alters			-.051	
Gender Heterogeneity of Alters			.022	
F	1.865*	3.943***	3.500***	4.254***
Adjusted R Square	.037	.124	.138	.145
Change in Adj. R Square from Model 1		.087***	.101**	.108***
Change in Adj. R Square from Model 2			.014	.021**

†† significance tests on control variables are two-tailed tests, all others are one-tailed tests - * p < .05 ** p < .01 *** p < .001

n = 250

opportunities *since firm founding* (including the opportunity for their current firm). Thus, it does not directly match the same time frame as the number of ideas recognized in the past year (except for entrepreneurs whose firms were founded in 1997). The total number of alters variable is a representation of the size of an entrepreneur's social network and the propensity to use the network to recognize opportunities (in other words, how "networked" an entrepreneur is). An individual who has utilized eight alters to recognize opportunities is more networked than an individual who has used only one. While there is a dynamic component to social networks as individual alters change over time, the overall size and composition (types of individuals, i.e., race, gender, age, etc.) of the network remains fairly stable (Davern, 1997). In this study, this is partially supported by the fact that there is no significant correlation between the age of the firm and the square root of the number of alters identified. If there was a change in the number of alters over time, we would expect a significant correlation to exist.

Based on the results presented in Model 1 on Table 16, we can see that the set of control variables produced a regression model that was significant ($F = 1.865, p < .05$). The next step of the analyses was testing the effects of the independent variables related to social network size and other network characteristics on square root of the numbers of ideas identified using hierarchical regression. As seen in Table 16, the size of an entrepreneur's social network plays an important part in the identification of new venture ideas (see Model 2, on Table 16). Adding the total number of alters significantly (p < .001) improved the regression model over Model 1 (just the control variables). Model 2 resulted in an adjusted R^2 of .124 ($F = 3.943, p < .001$). The standardized regression coefficient for number of new alters was also highly significant ($\beta = .304, p < .001$). Thus, a one standard deviation change in the number of alters in the social network would result in a .304 standard deviation change in the square root of the number of new venture ideas identified by the entrepreneur. These results provide strong support for Hypothesis 1a.

Model 3 shows the results of testing the importance of (1) the number of weak ties, (2) the number of structural holes, and (3) the racial and gender heterogeneity of the entrepreneur's network to the square root of the number of new venture ideas identified. Hypothesis 6a was supported based on the fact that the standardized regression coefficient for number of weak ties was significant and positive in Model 3 (β = .142, p < .05). However, Hypotheses 8a, 9a, and 10a were not supported as the regression coefficients for number of structural holes, racial heterogeneity of the alters and gender heterogeneity of the alters were not significant.

Model 3 was not a significant improvement over Model 2; however, by adding only the number of weak ties to Model 2, Model 4 was a significant (p < .01) improvement over Model 2, and it represents the most parsimonious regression model (Adjusted R^2 = .145, F = 4.254, p < .001).

8.2 EXAMINING THE NUMBERS OF NEW VENTURE OPPORTUNITIES RECOGNIZED

Hypotheses 1b, 6b, 8b, 9b, and 10b were also tested using hierarchical regression analyses. The square root transform of the number of opportunities recognized in the last year was regressed on eleven control variables and then on the independent variables. The square root transform was chosen for the same reasons given in the regression models described in the prior section. Table 17 summarizes statistical results for tests of the effects of various independent variables on the numbers of new venture opportunities entrepreneurs recognized in the last year.

Based on the results presented in Model 1 on Table 17, we can see that the individual control variables taken as a group were not significant predictors of the square root of the number of opportunities recognized at even the p < .10 level. The next step of the analyses was testing the effects of the independent variables related to social network size and other characteristics on numbers of opportunities recognized using hierarchical regression. Once again, the results indicate that an entrepreneur's social network plays an important part in the recognition of new venture opportunities (see Table 17).

The square root of the number of new venture opportunities recognized in the last year was regressed on the control variables and then on the number of alters who were identified by respondent entrepreneurs as individuals who helped them recognize potential new venture opportunities (see Model 2 on Table 17). Adding the number of alters to the model significantly (p < .001) improved the regression model over Model 1 (just the control variables). Model 2 resulted in an adjusted R^2 of .070 (F = 2.557, p < .01).

Table 17. Results of Regression Analyses for theSquare Root of the Number of New Venture Opportunities Recognized by Resppondents in the Last Year

Variable[++]	Model 1	Model 2	Model 3	Model 4
		Hyp. 1b	Hyp. 6b, 8b, 9b, 10b	BEST FIT/Hyp. 6b
	Beta	Beta	Beta	Beta
Controls				
Age	−.009	.016	−.009	−.013
Firm Age	.002	.024	.025	.026
Immigrant	−.056	−.083	−.076	−.074
Education	−.071	−.060	−.049	−.018
Business Major	−.099	−.107	−.099	−.089
Engineering/Science Major	−.160*	−.166*	−.162*	−.156*
Liberal Arts Major	.021	.013	.004	.013
Race-Asian (Indian/Oriental)	−.134[+]	−.135[+]	−.141[+]	−.135[+]
Race-Other (Black/Hispanic/Other)	−.093	−.104[+]	−.102	−.095[+]
Gender	−.017	−.003	−.012	−.007
Prior Experience	.016	−.029	−.020	−.016

Table 17. (Continued)

Variable[††]	Model 1	Model 2	Model 3	Model 4
		Hyp. 1b	Hyp. 6b, 8b, 9b, 10b	BEST FIT/Hyp. 6b
	Beta	Beta	Beta	Beta
Total Number of Alters Identified		.239***	.205**	.216***
Number of Weak Ties			.108†	.122*
Number of Structural Holes			.033	
Racial Heterogeneity of Alters			.033	
Gender Heterogeneity of Alters			.010	
F	1.406	2.557**	2.167**	2.647**
Adjusted R Square	.018	.070	.070	.080
Change in Adj. R Square from Model 1		.052***	.052***	.062***
Change in Adj. R Square from Model 2			.000	.010*

[††] significance tests on control variables are two-tailed tests, all others are one-tailed tests - † p < .10 * p < .05 ** p < .01 ***
p < .001
n = 250

The standardized regression coefficient for number of new alters was also highly significant and positive ($\beta = .239, p < .001$). These results provide support for Hypothesis 1b.

Model 3 on Table 17 shows the results of testing the importance of (1) the number of weak ties, (2) the number of structural holes, and (3) the racial and gender heterogeneity of the entrepreneur's social network to the square root of the number of new venture opportunities recognized. Hypothesis 6b was weakly supported based on the finding that the standardized regression coefficient for number of weak ties was marginally significant and positive in Model 3 ($\beta = .108, p < .10$). However, Hypotheses 8b, 9b, and 10b were not supported as the regression coefficients for number of structural holes, racial heterogeneity of the alters and gender heterogeneity of the alters were not significant.

Model 3 was not a significant improvement over Model 2; however, by adding only the number of weak ties to Model 2, Model 4 was a significant ($p < .05$) improvement over Model 2. It also supports Hypothesis 6b as the standardized regression coefficient for the number of weak ties is significant ($\beta = .122, p < .05$). Thus, Model 4 represents the most parsimonious regression model (Adjusted $R^2 = .080, F = 2.647, p < .01$).

8.3 EFFECTS OF NETWORK SIZE ON NUMBERS OF OPPORTUNITIES PURSUED

Hypothesis 2 proposed that entrepreneurs who utilize their social networks to recognize opportunities will pursue (invest time and money) more entrepreneurial opportunities than those who recognize opportunities individually. The square root of the number of new venture opportunities pursued in the last year was regressed on the control variables and then on the total number of alters identified. Hierarchical regression was again used to test the hypothesis and the number of opportunities pursued was transformed using the square root function (Agresti and Finlay, 1986; Cohen and Cohen, 1975; Norusis, 1991).

In addition, the hypothesis was tested by comparing the non-transformed mean number of opportunities pursued in the last year for solo entrepreneurs (those who did not indicate that any alters helped them recognize opportunities) and network entrepreneurs (those who indicated that at least one alter helped them recognize opportunities) using a *t*-test comparison. It was hypothesized that the mean number of opportunities pursued would be significantly higher for network entrepreneurs.

Table 18 summarizes the results of the regression models used to test Hypothesis 2 and Model 2 provides support for the hypothesis (Adjusted R^2 = .032, F = 1.691, p < .10). The standardized regression coefficient (β = .149) for number of alters was significant at the p < .01 level, after entering the control variables and entering the number of alters into the regression equation significantly (p < .05) explains 1.8 percent more variance than Model 1 (just the control variables).

Table 18. Results of Regression Analyses for theSquare Root of the Number of New Venture Opportunities Pursued (Invested Time and/or Money) by Respondents in the Last Year

Variable[++]	Model 1	Model 2
		Hyp. 2
	Beta	Beta
Controls		
Age	.013	.029
Firm Age	−.024	−.011
Immigrant	.038	.021
Education	.041	.048
Business Major	−.128[+]	−.133[+]
Engineering/Science Major	−.124[+]	−.127[+]
Liberal Arts Major	−.001	.006
Race - Asian (Indian/Oriental)	−.138[+]	−.139[+]
Race - Other (Black/Hispanic/Other)	−.087	−.094
Gender	.010	.019
Prior Experience	.029	.001
Total Number of Alters Identified		.149**
F	1.332	1.691[+]
Adjusted R Square	.014	.032
Change in Adjusted R Square from Model 1		.018*

[++] significance tests on control variables are two-tailed tests, main effect is a one-tailed test - [+] p < .10 * p < .05 ** p < .01

n = 250

In addition to the regression analysis, *t*-tests of the mean numbers of opportunities pursued were compared between solo entrepreneurs and network entrepreneurs. As seen in Table 19, there was a significant difference in the mean number of opportunities pursued by each group ($p < .05$). And as hypothesized, network entrepreneurs pursued a greater number of opportunities (1.9 vs. 1.2 for solo entrepreneurs). This result provides further support for Hypothesis 2.

8.4 EFFECTS OF NETWORK SIZE AND CHARACTERISTICS ON RANGE OF OPPORTUNITIES RECOGNIZED

Similar to Hypothesis 2, Hypothesis 3 proposed that entrepreneurs who utilized their social networks to recognize opportunities would recognize a wider range of entrepreneurial opportunities than those who recognize opportunities individually. The range of opportunities was operationalized by identifying the number of new venture opportunities the entrepreneur recognized that were unrelated to his/her current firm in the last year. In addition, the number of unrelated opportunities was transformed using

Table 19. A Comparison of the Number of Opportunities Pursued and Number of Opportunities Unrelated to the Current Business for Solo Entrepreneurs vs. Network Entrepreneurs (Supplementary Empirical Tests of Hypotheses 2 and 3)

Entrepreneur Type (n)	Number of Opportunities Pursued*	Number of Opportunities Unrelated to Current Business*
Solo Entrepreneurs (21)	1.2	0.6
Network Entrepreneurs (232)	1.9	1.3

* $p < .05$
n = 253

the square root function to better achieve a normal distribution of the residuals (Agresti and Finlay, 1986; Cohen and Cohen, 1975; Norusis, 1991). The square root of the number of new venture opportunities which were not related to the entrepreneur's current business was regressed on the control variables and then on the total number of alters identified.

In addition, the hypothesis was tested by comparing the mean number of opportunities recognized in the last year that are unrelated to the current firm (non-transformed) for solo entrepreneurs and network entrepreneurs using a *t*-test comparison. It was hypothesized that the mean number of unrelated opportunities to be significantly higher for network entrepreneurs.

Table 20 summarizes the results of the regression model (see Model 2) which provide support for Hypothesis 3. The standardized regression coefficient ($\beta = .129$) for the total number of alters was significant at the $p < .05$ level after entering the control variables.

In addition to the regression analysis, the mean number of unrelated opportunities for solo entrepreneurs and network was compared. As seen in Table 19, network entrepreneurs recognized significantly ($p < .05$) more opportunities that were unrelated to entrepreneurs' current businesses (1.3 vs. 0.6 for solo entrepreneurs). This also supports Hypothesis 3.

8.5 ALERTNESS AND PRIOR EXPERIENCE LEVELS OF NETWORK ENTREPRENEURS

Hypotheses 4 and 5 proposed that the more "networked" the entrepreneur is, the less prior experience in the industry prior to firm founding he/she will have and the less alert to opportunities he/she will be, respectively. To test these hypotheses, regression tests were conducted (see Tables 21 and 22).

In Table 21, the results of the regression test shows that after controlling for the entrepreneur's age, education, and college major, as well as the age of the firm, the more networked an entrepreneur is, the more prior experience they had prior to firm founding ($p < .01$). The results in Table 22 show that the more networked an entrepreneur is, the more alert to opportunities he/she is ($p < .05$). These findings are contrary to Hypotheses 4 and 5, thus, they were not supported.

118 *Opportunity Recognition through Social Networks*

Table 20. Results of Regression Analyses for theSquare Root of the Number of New Venture Opportunities Recognized by Resppondents in the Last Year That Were Unrelated to their Current Business

Variable[++]	Model 1 Beta	Model 2 Hyp. 3 Beta
Controls		
Age	.104	.117
Firm Age	−.019	−.008
Immigrant	.075	.060
Education	.097	−.091
Business Major	.072	.068
Engineering/Science Major	.016	.013
Liberal Arts Major	.021	.017
Race - Asian (Indian/Oriental)	.069	.068
Race - Other (Black/Hispanic/Other)	.074	.068
Gender	.025	.033
Prior Experience	−.187*	−.211**
Total Number of Alters Identified	.129*	
F	1.145	1.396
Adjusted R Square	.006	.019
Change in Adj. R Square from Model 1		.013*

[++] significance tests on control variables are two-tailed tests, main effect is one-tailed test - [†] p <.10 * p < .05 ** p < .01

n = 250

8.6 Intention to Found a Firm and then Recognizing the Opportunity vs. Recognizing the Opportunity and then Founding a Firm

Based on social network theory and Bhave's (1994) model, Hypotheses 11a and 11b proposed that the more networked an entrepreneur is, the more likely he/she is to first recognize the opportunity and then found the firm, while less networked/solo entrepreneurs would be more likely to decide to found a business and then seek out an opportunity. The hypotheses were tested

Table 21. Results of Regression Test for the Years of Prior Experience of respondents: A Test of the Impact of Being More "Networked" (Having More Alters Who Provide Opportunities)

	Model 1	Model 2
		Hyp. 4
Variable	Beta	Beta
Controls		
Age	.573***	.572***
Firm Age	.023	.038
Education	−.062	−.050
Business Major	−.083	−.087
Engineering/Science Major	.069	.066
Liberal Arts Major	−.091	−.093
Total Number of Alters Identified		.147**
F	19.278***	18.119***
Adjusted R Square	.301	.320
Change in Adj. R Square from Model 1		.019*

Two-tailed tests - * p < .05 ** p < .01 *** p < .001
n = 255

Table 22. Results of Regression Test for Self-Perceived Alertness to Opportunities by Respondents: A Test of the Impact of Being More "Networked: (Having More Alters Who Provide Opportunities)

	Model 1
	Hyp. 5
Variable	Beta
Total Number of Alters Identified	.128*
F	4.184*
Adjusted R Square	.012

Two-tailed test - * p < .05
n = 255

using a logistic regression test and then a supplementary Chi-Square test.

Table 23 shows that there is no significant relationship between the number of alters in the social network and whether the entrepreneur first recognized the opportunity and founded a firm or first intended to found a firm and then recognized an opportunity. Summarizing the supplementary test, Table 24 shows the results of the Chi-Square test of solo vs. network entrepreneurs. Again, no support was found for Hypotheses 11a and 11b as there were no significant differences between the two groups. Most entrepreneurs first recognized new venture opportunities and then decided to start a business rather than first deciding to start a business and then searching for opportunities.

8.7 UTILIZING STRONG AND WEAK TIES TO RECOGNIZE OPPORTUNITIES

It was hypothesized that entrepreneurs who utilized both strong and weak ties to recognize the opportunities for their firms would have more successful firms than those who did not use a mix of strong and weak ties. The inverted-U relationship could not be

Table 23. Results of Regression Test for How the Firm was Founded: The Relationship Between Being More "Networked" (Having More Alters Who Provide Opportunities) and Whether the Entrepreneur First Decided to Found A Firm and then Recognized the Opportunity or Whether the Entrepreneur First Recognized the Opportunity and Then Decided to Found a Firm

	Model 1
	Hyp. 11a, 11b
Variable	Beta
Total Number of Alters Identified	.055
F	0.777
Adjusted R Square	.000

Two-tailed test - * p < .05
n = 255

Table 24. Chi Square Test of How the Firm Was Founded: Whether the Entrepreneur First decided to Found A Firm and Then Recognized an Opportunity or Whether the Entrepreneur First Recognized the Opportunity and Then Decided to Found A Firm (Supplementary Empirical Test of Hypotheses 11a and 11b)

	Solo Entrepreneurs	Network Entrepreneurs	Row Totals
Entrepreneur First Decided to Start Business	3 (2.7) 1.2%	28 (28.3) 10.9%	31 12.1%
Entrepreneur First Recognized Opportunity	19 (19.3) 7.4%	206 (205.7) 80.5%	225 87.9%
Totals	22 8.6%	234 91.4%	256 100.0%

Expected Counts are in parentheses
Note: There were no significant differences

tested because there were only four respondents who only used weak ties, and many respondents with only strong ties. Originally, Hypothesis 7 was going to be tested using a measure of tie-strength of all of the alters. This variable would have ranged from 0 (all weak tie alters) to 1 (all strong tie alters); however, because of the data collected there was a severe range restriction on tie strength. In order to perform an analysis, entrepreneurs were divided into two groups: those who used no ties or only strong or weak ties (n = 205) and those who used at least one strong tie and one weak tie to recognize opportunities (n = 51).

To test the hypothesis, the log transform of the annual revenues was regressed on the control variables and then on the mix of ties dummy variable (see Table 25). Support for Hypothesis 7 can be seen in Model 2 on Table 25. Utilizing a mix of strong and weak ties to recognize the opportunity for their firms was a significant predictor of the log of firm revenues (β = .115, p < .05). The overall model with control variables and the dummy coded variable for mixed ties was a significant improvement over Model 1 (Adjusted R^2 = .061, F = 2.252, p < .001) at the p < .05 level.

8.8 EFFECT OF OPPORTUNITY RECOGNITION THROUGH SOCIAL NETWORKS ON FIRM PERFORMANCE

Finally, Hypothesis 12 proposed that entrepreneurs who utilized their social networks to recognize opportunities for their firms would have more successful firms than those who did not. To test this hypothesis, hierarchical regression equations were tested. The log transform of annual firm revenues was regressed on the control variables, then on the total number of alters identified by the entrepreneur. The log transforms were performed to linearize the relationships between revenues/employees and the independent and control variables, and to better achieve a normal distribution of the residuals (Agresti and Finlay, 1986; Cohen and Cohen, 1975; Norusis, 1991). Table 25 summarizes the results of the hierarchical regression analysis.

In Table 25, after accounting for all of the control variables, an entrepreneur who used more network contacts to recognize opportunities was significantly (marginally) more likely to earn greater annual revenues (β = .097, p < .10).

Table 25. Results of Regression Analyses for Log of Annual Firm Revenues

Variable[++]	Model 1	Model 2
		Hyp. 7/Hyp. 12
	Beta	Beta
Controls		
Age	.009	.010
Firm Age	.010	.021
Immigrant	−.075	−.083
Education	.081	.105
Business Major	.222**	.216**
Engineering/Science Major	−.046	−.056
Liberal Arts Major	−.049	−.065
Race - Asian (Indian/Oriental)	−.032	−.047
Race - Other (Black/Hispanic/Other)	−.041	−.042
Gender	−.106†	−.113†
Prior Experience	−.038	−.075
Total Number of Alters Identified		.097
Mix of Strong and Weak Ties Used to Recognize Opportunity for Firm (Dummy)		.115*
F	2.044*	2.252***
Adjusted *R* Square	.044	.061
Change in Adjusted *R* Square from Model 1		.015*

[++] significance tests on control variables are two-tailed tests, all others are one-tailed tests

† $p < .10$ * $p < .05$ ** $p < .01$ *** $p < .001$

n = 252

8.9 SUMMARY OF RESULTS FOR TESTS OF HYPOTHESES

Overall, the results indicated support for eight of the eighteen hypotheses. Table 26 restates the hypotheses and summarizes the results of the empirical tests of the hypotheses. The next chapter provides a more thorough discussion of the results described in this chapter and throughout the study. In Chapter 10, other significant results from supplementary statistical analyses are presented.

Table 26. Summary of Resulting Empirical Tests of Hypotheses

Hypothesis	Supported?
1a. *The greater the number of social network contacts an entrepreneur uses as idea identification sources, the greater the number of new venture ideas the entrepreneur will identify.*	Yes Table 16
1b. *The greater the number of social network contacts an entrepreneur uses as opportunity recognition sources, the greater the number of new venture opportunities the entrepreneur will recognize.*	Yes Table 17
2. *The greater the number of social network contacts an entrepreneur uses as opportunity recognition sources, the greater the number of new venture opportunities the entrepreneur will pursue.*	Yes Tables 18, 19
3. *The greater the number of social network contacts an entrepreneur uses as opportunity recognition sources, the wider the range of new venture opportunities the entrepreneur will recognize.*	Yes Tables 19, 20
4. *Entrepreneurs who utilize social network contacts to recognize the new venture opportunities for their businesses will have less personal experience in the industry than those entrepreneurs who recognize new venture opportunities individually.*	No Table 21 (Significant Contrary Results)
5. *Entrepreneurs who recognize new venture opportunitiesthrough their social network contacts will perceive themselves as less sensitive or alert to opportunities than those entrepreneurs who recognize opportunities individually.*	No Table 22 (Significant Contrary Results)
6a. *The number of new venture ideas identified by entrepreneurs will be positively related to the number of weak ties in their social networks.*	Yes Table 16
6b. *The number of new venture opportunities recognized by entrepreneurs will be positively related to the number of weak ties in their social networks.*	Yes Table 17

Table 26. (Continued)

Hypothesis	Supported?
7. Entrepreneurs who utilize a mix of both strong and weak ties will recognize more successful new venture opportunities than those who utilize only strong or only weak ties, or no alters at all.	Yes Table 25
8a. The number of new venture ideas identified by the entrepreneur will be positively related to the number of structural holes in their network.	No Table 16
8b. The number of new venture opportunities recognized by the entrepreneur will be positively related to the number of structural holes in their network.	No Table 17
9a. Entrepreneurs who have more racially heterogeneous sources in their social network will identify more new venture ideas than those who have more racially homogeneous alters.	No Table 16
9b. Entrepreneurs who have more racially heterogeneous opportunity sources in their social network will recognize more new venture opportunities than those who have more racially homogeneous alters.	No Table 17
10a. Entrepreneurs who have more gender heterogeneous opportunity sources in their social network will identify more new venture ideas than those who have more gender homogeneous alters.	No Table 26
10b. Entrepreneurs who have more gender heterogeneous opportunity sources in their social network will recognize more new venture opportunities than those who have more gender homogeneous alters.	No Table 27
11a. An entrepreneur who first chooses to start a business and then recognizes the opportunity for the business is less likely to have used his/her social network to recognize the opportunity.	No Tables 23, 24
11b. An entrepreneur who first recognizes the opportunity for his/her business is more likely to have used his/her social network to recognize the opportunity.	No Tables 23, 24
12. The greater the number of social network contacts anentrepreneur uses as opportunity recognition sources, the more successful his/her firm will be.	Yes, Marginal Table 25

CHAPTER 9

Discussion of Empirical Results and Research Model

Overall, the results of this study indicate that social networks play an important part in the opportunity recognition process of information technology consulting entrepreneurs. In Chapter 7, empirical support showed that social network contacts are important to idea identification as 33 percent of respondent entrepreneurs cited business associates as the source for the idea for their current firm and 19 percent cited friends and family. In total, approximately 42 percent indicated that they had obtained the idea for their business from business associates, friends, or family. The percentage is consistent with two other empirical studies which studied social network information sources for new venture ideas (Hills et al., 1997; Koller, 1988). The results in Chapter 7 also show that entrepreneurs with new venture ideas contacted potential clients/customers (50 percent), discussed their ideas with friends and family (46.5 percent), and/or sought out information/feedback from business associates (52 percent) before founding their firm. In fact, 75 percent of the respondent entrepreneurs marked at least one of the above social network activities as being part of their opportunity recognition processes. This extends the findings of Hills et al. (1997) and Koller (1988) which focused on idea identification, to show the clear importance of social networks to opportunity recognition.

In Chapter 8, multivariate heirarchical and logistic regression analyses showed that after accounting for eleven control variables, social networks significantly explained additional variance in the number of ideas and opportunities recognized, the number of opportunities pursued, the number of opportunities unrelated to the entrepreneur's current business, and size of the firm. These results provide the *first empirical support for the importance of network characteristics other than social network size to idea identification and opportunity recognition.* The strongest finding is that weak ties play a significant role in the identification of ideas and recognition of opportunities.

However, while many of the results were statistically significant, some of them were not as strong as expected. Several factors may have tempered the results. First, in order to focus the analysis to salient alters of interest in this study, entrepreneurs were asked to only provide information about people in their social network who helped them recognize opportunities, but the ideal study would examine the entirety of an entrepreneur's social network (not just those who helped them recognize opportunities). Despite its advantages, the limitation of the ego-network method is that it does not give a complete picture of an individual's network structure and composition (Wasserman and Faust, 1994), rather, it provides an accurate representation of an individual's overall network (Burt, 1984; Marsden, 1987; Wellman, 1993).

Another factor to consider is that an extensive name generator was not used (see Burt, 1992; p. 123) to prompt entrepreneurs to think about all of the alters who helped them recognize opportunities. It is likely that the entrepreneurs in this study did not fully consider all of the people who had influenced their opportunity recognition processes. The reason for not including a full-page name generator was the time and effort that would have been required of entrepreneurs. Adding an additional page to the questionnaire and requiring entrepreneurs to read through a full page of text and would have significantly reduced the response rate.

Additionally, the total number of alters is probably biased downward and toward strong ties (see Burt, 1986). Huang and Tausig (1990) discussed the use of ego-network interview question items on the 1985 General Social Survey.[1] They described the bias toward strong ties as a result of the limited name generator. They also described another, similar sociological study (the Northern California Community Study) which used ego-network items but included a more extensive name generator. That study resulted in mean network sizes of 18.5 alters with as many as 67 people being cited. Burt (1992) achieved much higher network sizes, in part, by using structured interviews and name generator items. Finally, the choice of information technology consultants for the study sample may have impacted results. It is possible that because of the prevalence of networking within the culture of information technology firms, the use of social networks in the opportunity recognition processes of entrepreneurs in this sample did not explain much unique variance. With most respondents in the sample using their social networks, the sample was relatively homogenous. However, the fact that there are significant findings provide support for the importance of social networks to entrepreneurial opportunity recognition.

The study of other samples of entrepreneurs from other industries and methods which allow for more in-depth study of an entrepreneurs' social networks, such as qualitative data gathering interviews, may lead to more significant findings (and more variance explained) related to the importance of the social network to opportunity recognition. But the use of the selected method allowed for an efficient, wide-ranging, and cost effective method of gathering information about entrepreneurs' social networks. And, there were significant findings consistent with many of the hypotheses. These are discussed further in the following sections.

9.1 SIZE OF AN ENTREPRENEUR'S SOCIAL NETWORK

Social encounters are a source of venture ideas (Christensen and Peterson, 1990), and thus, can lead to opportunity recognition. As Simon (1976) points out, individuals are limited in their ability to process and store information, which results in bounded rationality. The results of this study support the concept that an entrepreneur's social network can help expand the boundaries of rationality. The larger an entrepreneur's social network, the more access to information he/she has that can lead to new venture ideas and opportunities. Empirical support was found for this proposition in this study as almost nine percent of the variance in number of ideas identified was explained by the number of alters identified as important to opportunity recognition. In addition, over five percent of the variance in number of opportunities was explained by social network size. And significant percentages of the variances in the number of opportunities pursued and in the range of opportunities recognized were explained by the total number of alters.

In addition, social networks can improve the knowledge base of individuals by providing access to knowledge not contained by the individual. This knowledge expansion provides a stronger basis from which to determine a course of action (i.e., is an idea worth pursuing toward the recognition of an opportunity, and/or should an opportunity be pursued toward firm founding). By asking another person to assess the quality of a new venture idea entrepreneurs may be able to verify that the idea is in fact a true opportunity (or, just as important, not an opportunity). The outside alter may point out issues or features of the idea that need further consideration. In some cases, only when the issues have been addressed can the opportunity be recognized. Thus, the network can act as a "sounding board" which can help to focus ideas into opportunities.

9.2 EFFECT OF WEAK TIES

Weak ties serve as important sources of information within one's network. As discussed in Chapter 4, there is an upper bound limit on the number of close contacts one may physically interact with because of the maintenance costs associated with strong-tie relationships; however, it is possible for individuals to have many weak ties within their social networks. Additionally, as Granovetter (1973) points out, weak ties in an entrepreneur's social network provide more unique information. Using the example of an academic conference, an entrepreneurship researcher may meet dozens of weak-tie alters (other researchers whom he/she meets for the first time at the conference). These weak-tie alters may have a wealth of unique information that may spark an idea that leads to a new vein of research. The same can be true of would-be entrepreneurs. The mere interaction with others outside one's normal routine can lead an individual to identify new venture ideas and new financial opportunities.

Support was found here for Granovetter's (1973) "strength of weak ties" argument. As predicted, the number of weak ties within an entrepreneur's network is a significant predictor of the number of new venture ideas identified and new venture opportunities recognized. The total unique variance explained in number of ideas by weak ties was over two percent and for number of opportunities was one percent. These are conservative percentages because, again, specific information about only five alters within the entrepreneurs' networks were collected and there often tends to be a bias toward strong tie alters when using the ego-network method (Burt, 1986; Huang and Tausig, 1990; Marsden, 1987). Since there is the bias toward strong ties when the ego-network limits the extended data information to only five alters, one might conclude that those entrepreneurs who did specify that a weak tie(s) had helped them recognize opportunities have more weak ties in their overall social network than those who did not report using weak ties. In any event, the addition of weak ties to the regression models looking at numbers of opportunities and ideas significantly improved the regression models and that the regression coefficients in the models for weak ties were significant.

9.3 BENEFIT OF HAVING A MIX OF STRONG AND WEAK TIES

Based on Uzzi's (1996) findings, it was hypothesized that entrepreneurs are best served by utilizing both strong and weak ties to identify opportunities. Strong ties can provide more personal information which can be trusted and which reduces the need to do follow up research. Weak ties, on the other hand, can be greater in number and, as discussed above, provide more unique opportunities. While both strong and weak ties are important and can offer relevant information that leads to the recognition of a new venture opportunity, each type of tie can also offer different benefits. Consistent with the hypothesis, results showed that those entrepreneurs who utilized a mix of strong and weak ties to help them recognize the opportunity for their firm were more successful, in terms of annual revenues, than those who did not use anyone, or who used only strong or only weak ties.

Entrepreneurship is often a turbulent process, particularly during the early stages of new venture formation. In order to better cope with the uncertainty, an entrepreneur may need the social support of friends and family. The business idea may not be an opportunity for an individual if the person does not have the social support of close friends and/or family. Dyer (1992) found that some potential entrepreneurs were discouraged from founding their companies by family members because of the financial uncertainty and potential burden for the family to bear. To this end, Johannisson (1987) has argued that an entrepreneur's personal contacts can provide social support, a safety net, which allows the entrepreneur to break social norms in the process of risk-taking. For example, an entrepreneur may not consider a new venture idea an opportunity for a new venture if his wife does not support him. The opportunity may not exist for this individual because of personal background conditions.

By using strong and weak ties in the opportunity recognition process, an entrepreneur can gain the best of both worlds. The entrepreneur can use the wider range of experience and knowledge from weak ties, but benefit from the more trusted advice of close friends and family. Bianchi (1995) described a case in which the entrepreneur lay all of the groundwork for his new firm by speaking informally with clients about the possibility of using another firm. In addition, he selected three senior-level employees at the existing firm, and together the four of them met secretly during off-hours for two months prior to founding to discuss logistics and select other employees to take with them. The new firm was even able to secure a new client-server relationship with the larger "parent" company through the entrepreneur's contacts at his former firm. All of these preliminary informal discussions with strong ties (senior-level employees) and weak ties (future clients) helped to turn the business idea into an opportunity and reduce the subsequent liability of newness for the new firm. Based on the results of this study, entrepreneurs who utilize both strong and weak ties will be more likely to have more successful firms.

9.4 SOCIAL NETWORKS, OPPORTUNITY RECOGNITION, AND PERFORMANCE

Although there is a leap from opportunity recognition to firm performance since a myriad of post-founding factors such as financing, management, and marketing will play a role, it has been argued that the quality of the opportunity will have a direct impact on the success or failure of the business (Gaglio and Taub, 1992). Support is found for the concept that those entrepreneurs who use their social networks to recognize opportunities have more successful firms in this study. However, it is likely that those individuals who have a proclivity to use their networks to recognize their opportunities are more likely to use their networks for other business issues, such as marketing, management, and financing.

From a network perspective, researchers have argued and empirically demonstrated that size and interconnectivity of an entrepreneur's social network significantly affects new firm performance (e.g., Aldrich et al., 1987; Hansen, 1995; Nohria, 1992). These arguments have been based on the premise that networks facilitate the exchange of needed resources. In this study, being more networked is indicative of individuals who are more likely to discuss and develop their opportunities with the help of outside business and social contacts. Thus, these results should be taken in context, particularly given the fact that while the amount of variance explained in firm revenues from being more networked is significant, it is only 1.5 percent.

9.5 STRUCTURAL HOLES AND ALTER HETEROGENEITY

Based on the results in this study, there were no significant benefits from having more structural holes or more heterogeneous networks as measured in this study. However, this should be clarified. An individual's social network can include dozens or even hundreds of alters. This could result in hundreds of structural holes within the network; however, through the ego-network method employed in this study, only the number of holes between, and heterogeneity of, five alters could be determined. The maximum number of holes in this study was 10, but given that there tends to be a bias toward strong ties when using an ego-network survey, we would expect that there would be fewer structural holes within the network of identified alters than other parts of the respondents' networks. Five alters may not be sufficient to fully assess the importance of structural holes to opportunity recognition.

In addition, approximately 83 percent of the respondents were White and 86 percent were male. Thus, the homogeneity of the entrepreneurs tended to limit the amount of heterogeneity in the alters, as alters tend to be similar to the ego (Marsden, 1987). In fact, most of the entrepreneurs only listed white male alters. Thus, there was no heterogeneity to examine. Had information about the race and gender of more alters been gathered, and/or had there been a more racially and gender diverse sample of entrepreneurs, there may have been more significant findings.

9.6 DISCUSSION OF OTHER RESULTS

It was hypothesized that there would be significant differences in the levels of alertness to opportunities and in the prior experience levels of entrepreneurs between network and solo entrepreneurs. This study found that significant relationships existed, but not in the direction expected. More networked entrepreneurs had more industry experience prior to founding their firm and viewed themselves as more alert to opportunities than less networked entrepreneurs. It was proposed that they would have less—using the experience and alertness of their social network contacts to their benefit. These results indicate that social networks grow as a result of working in an industry and that as individuals gain experience, they become more alert to possible opportunities in the industry. The fact that all of the entrepreneurs in this study were information technology (IT) consulting entrepreneurs may have played a role in the lack of significant findings with respect to differences in alertness and prior experience. The dynamic, rapidly changing power of IT may require that entrepreneurs in this industry be highly sensitive to opportunities. As quickly as technology changes, entrepreneurs must continue to innovate to keep up with, and perhaps slightly ahead of, competition in order to succeed.

Based on Bhave's model of opportunity recognition, solo entrepreneurs were expected to be individuals who first decided to start a business and then sought out opportunities for their would-be business. On the other hand, network entrepreneurs were believed to be more likely to first recognize an opportunity and then found a business to take advantage of the opportunity. But there were no differences in when the opportunity was recognized with respect to the timing of the intention to found a firm. Most entrepreneurs from *both* groups first recognized the opportunities for their businesses and then founded their firm. Again, this may be a product of the chosen survey sample. The IT industry is a high growth industry without barriers to entry. Opportunities abound because the population density (Hannan and Freeman, 1977) of IT firms is low, and the carrying capacity (Carroll and Hannan, 1989) is high. As the industry matures there may be a need for new firms to become specialists (Lambkin, 1988; Romanelli, 1989) in order to survive, which may lead to significantly more systematic search for opportunities and significant findings with respect to solo versus network entrepreneurs.

9.7 THE EFFECT OF COFOUNDERS

Before discussing limitations of this study, the analysis of cofounders in this study should be clarified. The reader will notice that in the published tables and discussion throughout the study there is no real discussion of cofounders. Initially, the number of cofounders was used as a control variable in the regression analyses. During early analysis, regression models were run with the number of cofounders included; however, cofounders were not a significant predictor of number of new venture ideas identified, opportunities recognized, or other dependent variables in this study. After careful review of the more specific network data gathered for up to five alters, it was determined that most entrepreneurs with cofounders included their cofounders in their identified alters who were important to their recognition of opportunities. Thus, the number of cofounders was accounted for in the total number of alters variable. Since the number of cofounders, by itself, was not a significant predictor of ideas or opportunities, and was accounted for in total number of alters variable, it was not used in the analyses.

9.8 DISCUSSION OF MODELS DEVELOPED IN THIS STUDY

The model of entrepreneurial opportunity (Figure 3) and the basic research model (Figure 4) used in this study were based largely on the discussions of Timmons (1990; 1994a; 1994b) and Long and McMullan (1984). The models developed in this study are broad models and it should be noted that in no way do the models exclude the constructs specified in the Bhave (1994), Gaglio and Taub (1992), or Christensen et al. (1994) models. For example, the latter two models were linear processes that are represented in the model of entrepreneurial opportunity by the broad environmental and individual background variables. Further, Bhave's discussion and illustration of externally-stimulated and internally-stimulated opportunity recognition could be represented by the path from the environment and individual to idea identification. While there are similarities between the model of opportunity developed in this study and the other models, the current model differs in the illustration and discussion of the explicit mediation effect of idea identification between the combination of environmental and individual factors and opportunity recognition. In addition, the model of entrepreneurial opportunity in this study discusses the moderating effect of the environment and the individual factors of the entrepreneur on the relationship between idea identification and opportunity recognition.

Opportunity recognition is a complex process and the models developed in this study were purposefully parsimonious in order to direct the reader and survey respondents to the key elements of the opportunity recognition process. The research model (Figure 4) was a more basic representation of the model of an entrepreneurial opportunity (Figure 3). It was included on the questionnaire to explicitly frame the difference between new venture ideas and new venture opportunities. The validity of the model was shown by the responses to the three validity check questions (84 percent of respondents understood and agreed with the model), and the results detailed in Chapter 7 of this study demonstrate the clear distinctions between the idea and opportunity constructs. The research model may prove to be the most important element of this study, because it can be (and arguably should be) used in any study of opportunity recognition to help study participants distinguish the two constructs (ideas and opportunities).

9.9 LIMITATIONS

The limitations of the ego-network method have already been discussed, as has the fact that a full name generator or name generator questions to prompt the respondent to consider all of the people in their social network who helped them identify new venture ideas and recognize new venture opportunities were not used. Two other issues that have not been discussed but that do bear mentioning are common method variance and the lack of independent corroborating measures of the strength of interpersonal relationships within the network. With respect to the latter, a respondent may have over or understated the strength of ties. And since all of the data were collected by a single questionnaire there is the potential for common method variance. For example, there may have been some systematic bias between respondents and non-respondents. However, as seen in Chapter 6, there was no difference in terms of annual revenues and number of employees between respondents and non-respondents. So while the chance that systematic bias does exist, the possibility is reduced based on the non-significant findings stated above.

Aside from issues related to the ego-network method and design, the primary limitation of this study is that the data used in the statistical analyses are cross-sectional. Causality can never truly be determined using a cross-sectional data. However, it seems unlikely that the number of new venture opportunities recognized would lead to an increase in the number of alters who helped the entrepreneur recognize the opportunity. The use of time series type questions make it easier to interpret the findings in a logical way such that causal relationships can be predicted, but ideally, a study that examines the process of opportunity recognition would examine individuals who intend to become entrepreneurs from pre-founding through opportunity recognition and firm founding. For obvious reasons, such an effort is difficult because not only does it demand that researchers identify nascent entrepreneurs prior to opportunity recognition, it requires them to keep track of all of the alters the individual contacts over time. Knowing that the opportunity recognition process can take months and even years (see Chapter 7) only further complicates matters. Again, the ego-network questionnaire provided a means of testing the importance of social networks at considerable cost and time savings. Since there were statistically significant findings, researchers can now test the hypotheses using more complete methods of measuring the size and composition of the social network. In addition, there will be followup questionnaires mailed to respondents in the future to better understand opportunity recognition processes over time.

This questionnaire included several retrospective items which may be subject to both memory recall issues and/or halo effects which change the way entrepreneurs remembered events of interest in this study. In order to minimize the potential error associated with memory loss, only firms that were founded in 1994 or later were selected.

9.10 CONCLUSIONS

These limitations not withstanding, the results of this study make a significant contribution to the opportunity recognition literature. As stated earlier, there is still relatively little empirical study of the antecedents to, and processes of, opportunity recognition. This study examined the theoretical models of opportunity recognition offered by researchers in the past and developed a working definition of entrepreneurial opportunity and a basic research model of the opportunity recognition process. This model allows researchers to study the differences between ideas and opportunities and may become an important tool in future opportunity recognition research, because of its parsimony and high validity.

In addition, this study is the first study to extensively study the specific role social networks play in the opportunity recognition process. The significant findings demonstrate support for the importance of social network characteristics and new directions for future entrepreneurship research are revealed. Future research needs are discussed more extensively in Chapter 11.

ENDNOTE

1. The General Social Survey (GSS) serves as a national resource for diverse academic interests. It is funded by the National Science Foundation (NSF) to gather sociological data from a representative cross section of the people of the United States. The data contained within the GSS include such things as general disposition (satisfaction, happiness, etc.), racial attitudes, political views, opinions on gender issues, as well as demographic information on each respondent. In the past, the GSS has been one of the most widely used data sources by sociologists to study characteristics of the U.S. population. The survey is conducted through personal interviews with several hundred respondents annually and is considered the premier national sociological survey of the United States (see Burt, 1984).

CHAPTER 10

Supplementary Analyses of Data

There were a number of relationships that were not specifically hypothesized, but which were tested in order to better understand opportunity recognition. This chapter presents the findings. First, *t*-test comparisons of demographic characteristics and questionnaire responses of study entrepreneurs and those who were deleted due to the lack of agreement/understanding with the idea and opportunity research model (validity check questions) are presented and discussed. Second, the relative importance of self-perceived alertness vs. social network characteristics to opportunity recognition is examined. Third, the effects of age and education heterogeneities of networks on opportunity recognition are tested. And finally, the chapter concludes with an exploratory factor analysis that presents three opportunity recognition factors.

10.1 DIFFERENCES BETWEEN STUDY SAMPLE AND RESPONDENTS WHO DID NOT AGREE WITH (OR UNDERSTAND) THE OVERARCHING RESEARCH MODEL

As discussed in Chapters 6 and 7, 47 entrepreneurs were removed from the analysis because they did not answer the validity check question consistently with the proposed basic model of opportunity recognition (see Figure 4). The model is largely based on Long and McMullan's (1984) model of opportunity recognition and Timmons' (1990; 1994a; 1994b) discussion of ideas and opportunities. Pre-test results and subsequent discussions with the eleven entrepreneurs who volunteered to pre-test the questionnaire also confirmed that entrepreneurs knew the difference between ideas and opportunities. The mail survey was designed such that entrepreneurs must agree with, and understand, the model. Thus, only entrepreneurs who responded to the validity check questions consistently with the model were included in the empirical tests of the hypotheses. Table 27 presents the demographic differences between the study sample of entrepreneurs who were included in the tests of hypotheses and those who were removed from the analysis based on the validity check questions.

In terms of demographic characteristics and firm characteristics of the two groups there was very little difference. The only significant difference was the amount of personal experience. Those who were included in the analyses had significantly less industry

Table 27. Demographic Comparison of Means Between Study Sample Entrepreneurs and Those Who Were Removed From the Analyses (Based on Validity Check Questions)

Item	Agreed[a]	Did Not Agree[b]
Age (years)	38.7	40.6
Age of the firm (years)	2.9	2.9
Number of cofounders	0.9	0.9
Education (scored on a 6-point Likert-type scale from 1=high school drop out to 6=graduate degree)	4.5	4.6
Number of businesses founded (Including current business)	1.9	1.8
Prior industry experience (years)	9.8[+]	11.9[+]
Number of Employees	10.8	6.3
Annual Revenues	$1,150,145	$662,108

[a] $N = 256$ (these were the entrepreneurs who were used to test hypotheses)
[b] $N = 47$ (these were the entrepreneurs who were excluded from analyses)
[+] $p < .10$

experience prior to founding their firms; however, it is not clear why there would be a difference, and indeed, the difference was only marginally significant ($p < .10$). None of the other characteristics were statistically different. Although the number of employees and firm revenues appear to be different, they were not. The mean number of employees and revenues of those who agreed with the model were affected by several outliers. A check of the median revenues also revealed that there was no significant difference between the two groups ($227,550—study sample vs. $220,000—excluded respondents).

Entrepreneurs were asked to indicate their level of agreement to a series of 18 statements regarding their satisfaction with their firm, their personal opinion of themselves, and issues related to opportunity recognition. Table 28 provides a listing of the items as they appeared in the questionnaire (they were questions 26–44 on the mail questionnaire) and the entrepreneur responses from each of the two groups.

Once again, it seems that there was very little difference between the two types of entrepreneurs. Those who were dropped from the analyses were significantly less likely to believe that immersion in an industry is a requirement to recognize opportunities in that industry. They were also marginally less likely to believe that "gut feel" was important and were less likely to indicate that they recognized a wider range of opportunities. It is possible that these individuals are more likely to undergo strategic planning for opportunities than those who were retained in the study. Those who did not agree may assess opportunities in a particular market area that they are comfortable in (more likely to recognize similar opportunities) without relying on gut feel. And rather than immerse themselves in the industry area, they may take more of a strategic planning approach. On the question of the importance of social networks, both groups agreed that social contacts are important to opportunity recognition.

Although the 47 entrepreneurs who were deleted from further study did not agree with the research model of opportunity recognition, comparisons to the entrepreneurs that were included in the study were made with respect to the reported numbers of ideas and opportunities recognized. Table 29 presents those results.

The entrepreneurs in the second group reported identifying significantly fewer venture ideas in the last year. It is not clear

Table 28. Comparison of Mean Responses Between Respondents Who Agreed With and Understood the Research Model to Those Who Did Not on a Variety of Factors

Item	Agreed[a]	Did Not Agree[b]
Sometimes I feel I don't have enough control over the direction my life is taking.	2.4	2.2
Success is a matter of hard work; luck has little or nothing to do with it.	3.3	3.2
I would never have started my business, if I knew then what I now know.	1.5	1.5
While going about routine day-to-day activities, I see potential new venture ideas all around me.	4.0	3.8
I often do financial calculations in my head when I see potential new venture ideas.	3.7	3.7
I have a special "alertness" or sensitivity toward new venture opportunities.	3.5	3.7
Recognizing opportunities is really several learning steps over time, rather than a "eureka" experience.	3.9	3.9
It is easier to see opportunities after you start a business and enter the market (as compared to before you start).	3.8	3.8
I can recognize potential new venture opportunities in industries where I have no personal experience.	3.3	3.5
Having the money to take advantage of an opportunity has little to do with *recognizing* an opportunity.	3.7	3.7
New venture ideas are a dime a dozen. Evaluation is the key to recognizing *good* opportunities.	4.0	3.8

Table 28. (Continued)

Item	Agreed[a]	Did Not Agree[b]
New venture ideas are a dime a dozen. Evaluation is the key to recognizing *good* opportunities.	4.0	3.8
Conducting formal market analyses is important to recognizing new venture opportunities.	3.2	3.2
Social contacts (friends, family, business contacts, etc.) are important to recognizing opportunities.	3.9[†]	3.7[†]
The new venture opportunities I haverecognized over the years havebeen mostly unrelated to each other.	2.7	2.5
"Seeing" potential new venture opportunities does *not* come very naturally to me.	2.2	2.3
Recognizing good opportunities usually requires "immersion" in a specific industry or marketplace.	3.0*	2.7*
If I recognize a good opportunity, I can raise the capital needed to take advantage of the opportunity.	3.2	3.1
"Gut feel" is important to recognizing opportunities.	3.8[†]	3.6[†]
Overall, I am satisfied with the growth and development of my firm.	3.8	3.7

NOTE: All responses were coded on a 5-point scale from 1=Strongly Disagree to 5=Strongly Agree (3=Neutral)
[a] $N = 256$ (these were the entrepreneurs who were used to test hypotheses)
[b] $N = 47$ (these were the entrepreneurs who were excluded from analyses)
* $p < .05$
† $p < .10$

Table 29. Mean Numbers of Ideas Identified and Opportunities Recognized for the Study Sample and Those Who Were Excluded From the Analyses

Item	Agreed[a]	Did Not Agree[b]
Ideas last month	2.4	2.1
Ideas last year	6.6*	5.3*
Opportunities last month	1.2	1.0
Opportunities last year	3.3	3.5

[a] $N = 253$ (these were the entrepreneurs who were used to test hypotheses)
[b] $N = 47$ (these were the entrepreneurs who were excluded from analyses)
* $p < .05$

whether they understood what the difference between an idea and opportunity was, so interpreting these results is problematic. On the questions of what activities they conducted to help them conceive of the idea for their business, and what they did to turn the idea into the opportunity for their business, there were again similarities to those individuals who understood and agreed with the model. Table 30 presents the reported idea sources (entrepreneurs could indicate more than one source), and Table 31 summarizes opportunity recognition activities.

The results show that business associates and friends or relatives were not cited as sources for ideas as often for the group of respondents who were dropped and they were less likely to discuss their ideas with friends and/or seek out advice from business associates. In addition, those who were dropped were more likely to have prepared financial statements and contacted potential clients, whereas the respondents who agreed with the research model were more likely to just know that their idea was an opportunity. These findings support the idea that the group that did not understand/agree with the model are strategic planners. They are more careful about how they assess their opportunities. However, while there were clearly some differences between the groups, the two groups appeared to be more similar than different.

Table 30. Where Entrepreneurs Obtain Their Ideas: Frequency Comparisons of Study Sample to Those Who Were Excluded From Analysis

Source	Agreed[a]	Did Not Agree[b]
Prior Experience	73.0%	76.6%
Business Associates	32.8%	23.4%
Saw a Similar Business	25.8%	21.3%
Friends or Relatives	19.1%	4.3%
Hobby/Personal Interest	17.2%	17.0%
Market Research	11.3%	12.8%
It Just Came to Mind	10.9%	8.5%
Magazine/Newspaper	2.3%	0.0%
Radio/Television	0.4%	4.3%
Other	4.7%	8.5%

[a] $N = 256$ (these were the entrepreneurs who were used to test hypotheses)
[b] $N = 47$ (these were the entrepreneurs who were excluded from analyses)

Table 31. Opportunity Recognition Activities: Frequency Comparison of Study Sample to Those Who Were Excluded From Analysis

Activity	Agreed[a]	Did Not Agree[b]
Sought out information/feedback from business associates	52.0%	46.8%
Contacted potential customers/clients	50.0%	59.6%
Discussed idea with friends/family members	46.5%	42.6%
Gathered information on competitors	33.6%	31.9%
None, just knew idea was an opportunity	33.2%	25.5%
Prepared financial statements	25.0%	38.3%
Other	3.5%	12.8%

[a] $N = 256$ (these were the entrepreneurs who were used to test hypotheses)
[b] $N = 47$ (these were the entrepreneurs who were excluded from analyses)

10.2 EXAMINING SOCIAL NETWORKS AND PERCEIVED ALERTNESS TO OPPORTUNITY RECOGNITION

The fundamental hypothesis of this study is that structural characteristics of the social networks of entrepreneurs are important for opportunity recognition. From the traditional individual "traits" perspective, a competing hypothesis could be that opportunity recognition is simply a result of more "opportunistic" individuals rather than social networks. This hypothesis was tested using a hierarchical regression model. First, the square root of the number of ideas identified in the last year was regressed on the 12 control variables and then on self-perceptions of opportunity alertness. Alertness was measured using a three item scale measure (alpha=.78). The question items were Questions 29, 31, and 40 from the questionnaire. Then, the total number of alters was added to the model, followed by the number of weak ties and structural holes. Table 32 summarizes the four regression models that examined the effects on the number of new venture ideas identified. The same procedure described above was also used to study the effects on the square root of new venture opportunities recognized in the last year. Table 33 presents the four regression models for opportunity recognition.

In Table 32 we see that self-perceptions of opportunity alertness was a highly significant predictor of the number of new venture ideas an entrepreneur recognized. Model 1 shows that, as a set, the individual control variables (age, gender, race, education, college major, immigrant, years of prior experience, and firm age) were significant in explaining 3.7 percent of the variance in the square root of new venture ideas ($F = 1.865, p < .05$).

In the second model, we can see the effect of Alertness. Model 2 significantly improved the regression model over Model 1 (just control variables). Model 2 resulted in an adjusted R^2 of .239 ($F = 7.556, p < .001$). The standardized regression coefficient for Alertness was .454 ($p < .001$). Thus, a one standard deviation change in Alertness will result in a .454 standard deviation change in the square root of the number of new venture ideas identified by the entrepreneur.

Models 3 and 4 added network characteristics to the regression model. The addition of the total number of alters identified resulted in an adjusted R^2 of .290 ($F = 9.729, p < .001$). Again, this

Table 32. Results of Regression Analyses for the Square Root of the Number of New Venture Ideas Identified by Respondents in the Last Year (Including Self-perception of Alertness)

Variable[++]	Model 1 Beta	Model 2 Beta	Model 3 Beta	Model 4 Beta
Controls				
Age	-.091	-.070	-.046	-.071
Firm Age	-.062	-.115	-.089	-.088
Immigrant	.041	.058	.030	.044
Education	-.035	-.031	-.021	.008
Business Major	-.045	-.064	-.070	-.069
Engineering/Science Major	-.060	-.037	-.045	-.046
Liberal Arts Major	-.053	-.110[†]	-.113[†]	-.124*
Race - Asian (Indian/Oriental)	-.178*	-.137*	-.142*	-.145*
Race - Other (Black/Hispanic/Other)	-.052	-.045	-.056	-.043
Gender	-.086	-.085	-.071	-.077
Prior Experience	-.020	.020	-.028	-.023

Table 32. (Continued)

Variable[++]	Model 1 Beta	Model 2 Beta	Model 3 Beta	Model 4 Beta
Self-Perceived Alertness		.454***	.416***	.415***
Total Number of Alters Identified			.236***	.224***
Number of Weak Ties				.152*
Number of Structural Holes				−.036
F	1.865*	7.556***	9.729***	8.280***
Adjusted R Square	.037	.239	.290	.304
Change in Adj. R Square from Model 1		.202***	.253***	.267***
Change in Adj. R Square from Model 2			.051***	.065**
Change in Adj. R Square from Model 3				.014[+]

[++] significance tests on control variables are two-tailed tests, all others are one-tailed tests

[+] $p < .10$
* $p < .05$
** $p < .01$
*** $p < .001$
n = 248

Table 33. Results of Regression Analyses for the Square Root of the Number of New Venture Opportunities Recognized by Respondents in the Last Year (Including Self-Perception of Alertness)

Variable	Model 1 Beta	Model 2 Beta	Model 3 Beta	Model 4 Beta
Controls				
Age	–.009	.007	.026	.007
Firm Age	.001	–.039	–.018	–.017
Immigrant	–.056	–.043	–.065	–.055
Education	–.071	–.068	–.060	–.051
Business Major	–.099	–.113[†]	–.118[†]	–.117[†]
Engineering/Science Major	–.160*	–.142*	–.149*	–.149*
Liberal Arts Major	.021	–.023	–.025	–.033
Race-Asian (Indian/Oriental)	–.134[†]	–.102	–.106	–.108
Race-Other (Black/Hispanic/Other)	–.093	–.087	–.096	–.087
Gender	–.017	–.017	–.006	–.010
Prior Experience	.016	.046	.008	.013

Table 33. (Continued)

Variable	Model 1 Beta	Model 2 Beta	Model 3 Beta	Model 4 Beta
Self-Perceived Alertness		.350***	.320***	.319***
Total Number of Alters Identified			.186**	.176*
Number of Weak Ties				.110*
Number of Structural Holes				–.023
F	1.406	4.295***	4.834***	4.411***
Adjusted R Square	.018	.137	.166	.170
Change in R Square from Model 1		.119***	.148***	.152***
Change in R Square from Model 2			.029**	.033*
Change in R Square from Model 3				.004

†† significance tests on control variables are two-tailed tests, all others are one-tailed tests

† p < .10
* p < .05
** p < .01
*** p < .001
n = 248

represented a better model and explained more variance (5.1 percent more) in the number of new venture ideas recognized. With the addition of weak ties and structural holes to the model (Model 4), we see that the model explains an additional 6.5 percent of the variance ($F = 8.985$, $p < .001$) in numbers of ideas over Model 2 (control variables and Alertness). However, Model 4 was not a significantly better model than Model 3.

Model 1 of Table 33 shows that the set of individual control variables was not significant in explaining variance in the square root of the numbers of new venture opportunities. In the second model, we can see the added effect of Alertness. Model 2 was a significantly improved regression model over Model 1. Model 2 resulted in an adjusted R^2 of .137 ($F = 4.295$, $p < .001$). The standardized regression coefficient for Alertness was .350 and was highly significant ($p < .001$). Thus, a one standard deviation change in Alertness will result in a .350 standard deviation change in the square root of the number of new venture opportunities recognized by the entrepreneur.

Models 3 and 4 added in the network effects to the regression model. The addition of the total number of alters identified resulted in an adjusted R^2 of .166 ($F = 4.834$, $p < .001$). Again, this represented a better model and explained significantly more variance (2.9 percent more) in the square root of the number of new venture opportunities recognized. With the addition of weak ties and structural holes to the model (Model 4), we see that there is no significant improvement over Model 3. Thus, adding both self-perceived alertness and network size significantly predicts the numbers of ideas identified and opportunities recognized. This demonstrates the importance of social networks to opportunity recognition by showing that even after accounting for self-perceptions of alertness, social networks still make a difference.

In future studies, the level of self-perceived alertness should be confirmed using alternative measures to test the validity and reliability of self-reports. It is possible that those individuals who say that they are more alert to opportunities may also overstate the number of opportunities they recognize. The self-perception of alertness may be an indicator of how highly individuals think of themselves. Further analyses of the data and the entrepreneurs in this sample is needed to test for bias in the self-reported levels of alertness. However, the results continue to support the concept that social networks play an important part in predicting the numbers of new venture ideas and opportunities recognized.

10.3 TESTS OF AGE AND EDUCATIONAL HETEROGENEITIES OF SOCIAL NETWORKS

In Chapter 8, it was reported that racial and gender heterogeneity did not impact idea identification or opportunity recognition. Supplementary tests were conducted to test the impact of age and educational heterogeneity. The square root of the number of new venture ideas identified in the last year was regressed on the control variables and then on the total number of alters identified, number of weak ties, and IQV's for age and education. A second set of regression equations were tested using the same method, replacing ideas with the square root of the number of new venture opportunities recognized.

Table 34 summarizes the results of the first regression model. There was no significant finding for the relationship between age and educational heterogeneities of social networks and idea identification. However, Table 35 shows that educational heterogeneity of the social network ($\beta=-.112$) was marginally significant at the $p < .05$ level. This indicates that as an entrepreneur's social network becomes more educationally diverse, the entrepreneur will recognize fewer opportunities. This finding is contrary to the expectations for heterogeneity of a network. The more heterogeneous the network, the more ideas and opportunities the entrepreneur should be able to recognize. It is possible that a diverse network of alters may pull the entrepreneur in many directions which reduces the number of opportunities that may be recognized. Further study is needed to better understand the negative effect.

10.4 OPPORTUNITY RECOGNITION FACTORS

One of the secondary aims of this research was to further develop a reliable set of opportunity recognition questionnaire items that might be used in future research. An attempt was made to identify opportunity recognition factors. An exploratory factor analysis was performed using varimax rotation on 16 questionnaire items which dealt with aspects of opportunity recognition perceptions

Table 34. Results of Regression Models for the Square Root of the Number of New Venture Ideas Identified by Respondents in the Last Year (Test of Age and Educational Heterogeneities of Network)

Variable[‡‡]	Model 1 Beta	Model 2 Beta	Model 3 Beta
Controls			
Age	−.091	−.058	−.084
Firm Age	−.062	−.035	−.036
Immigrant	.041	.006	.027
Education	−.035	−.021	.010
Business Major	−.045	−.056	−.051
Engineering/Science Major	−.060	−.068	−.068
Liberal Arts Major	−.053	−.063	−.072
Race-Asian (Indian/Oriental)	−.178*	−.180*	−.183*
Race-Other (Black/Hispanic/Other)	−.052	−.067	−.053
Gender	−.086	−.067	−.079
Prior Experience	−.020	−.077	.063

Table 34. (Continued)

Variable[††]	Model 1 Beta	Model 2 Beta	Model 3 Beta
Total Number of Alters Identified		.304***	.273***
Number of Weak Ties			.150**
Age Heterogeneity (IQV)			.029
Educational Heterogeneity (IQV)			−.055
F	1.865*	3.944***	3.737***
Adjusted *R* Square	.037	.124	.141
Change in Adj. *R* Square from Model 1		.087**	.104***
Change in Adj. *R* Square from Model 2			.017*

[††] significance tests on control variables and IQV variables are two-tailed tests, all others are one-tailed tests

[†] $p < .10$
* $p < .05$
** $p < .01$
*** $p < .001$
n = 250

Table 35. Results of Regresion Models for the Square Root of the Number of New Venture Opportunities Recognized by Respondents in the Last Year (Test of Age and Educational Heterogeneities of Network)

Variable[++]	Model 1 Beta	Model 2 Beta	Model 3 Beta
Controls			
Age	–.009	.016	.001
Firm Age	.002	.024	.023
Immigrant	–.056	–.083	–.056
Education	–.071	–.060	–.050
Business Major	–.099	–.107	–.104
Engineering/Science Major	–.160*	–.166*	–.162*
Liberal Arts Major	.021	.013	.005
Race-Asian (Indian/Oriental)	–.134[+]	–.135[+]	–.144[+]
Race-Other (Black/Hispanic/Other)	–.093	–.104[+]	–.093
Gender	–.017	–.003	–.008
Prior Experience	.016	–.029	–.009

Table 35. (Continued)

Variable[++]	Model 1 Beta	Model 2 Beta	Model 3 Beta
Total Number of Alters Identified		.239***	.218***
Number of Weak Ties			.096[+]
Age Heterogeneity (IQV)			–.016
Educational Heterogeneity (IQV)			–.112*
F	1.406	2.557***	2.517***
Adjusted R Square	.018	.070	.083
Change in Adj. R Square from Model 1		.052***	.065***
Change in Adj. R Square from Model 2			.013*

[++] significance tests on control variables and IQV variables are two-tailed tests, all others are one-tailed tests

[+] $p < .10$
* $p < .05$
** $p < .01$
*** $p < .001$
n = 250

and behaviors and satisfaction with the firm (questions 29–44, and 49). The factor analysis was performed on the full 303 entrepreneurs that responded to the survey. This was done because the items used in the factor analysis were not critically linked to the research model and there was little difference between the entrepreneurs who were eliminated from analyses and the study sample used to test the hypotheses (see Section 10.1).

Since this was an exploratory factor analysis, the analysis was performed using the 16 items, removed double loading items and items which fell into single item factors, and re-ran the factor analysis (Blalock, 1974; Child, 1990; Kim and Mueller, 1978). Primary emphasis was placed on interpretability and was left with a three factor solution that combined explained 57.4 percent of the variance. All three factors had eigenvalues over 1.0 and were above the point where the scree diagram flattened out. Table 36 shows the rotated principal factors solution and summarizes the three factors and the factor loadings of individual items.

Only one of the factors had an alpha above .70; however, for the purposes of this exploratory analyses several future research directions were found. Factor 1 entrepreneurs consisted of the "Opportunity Sensors" who perceived themselves to be highly sensitive to opportunities. In addition, entrepreneurs in this category are likely to perform financial calculations in their heads when they see potential new venture ideas. Clearly, these were individuals who demonstrated confidence in themselves and indicated that they were adept at recognizing opportunities. An example of this type of entrepreneur may be the stereotypical entrepreneur who continually identifies ideas for new venture opportunities. He is the one who walks into a restaurant, and realizes that the restaurant is doing great business, and then while sitting down quickly calculates how much it would cost to start such a business and how much he could make.

Although neither the second nor third factors had high internal reliability (both alphas were under .60), they did represent two different types of entrepreneur and may be useful for future scale development. Factor 2 entrepreneurs were entrepreneurs who were satisfied with the growth and development of their businesses and who had confidence that if they recognized a good opportunity they could raise the capital needed to take advantage of it. We might think of these entrepreneurs as the "Opportunity

Table 36. Results of Factor Analysis of Opportunity Recognition Items

	Factors*		
ITEM	1	2	3
While going about routine day-to-day activities, I see potential new venture ideas all around me.	.74		
I often do financial calculations in my head when I see potential new venture ideas.	.69		
I have a special "alertness" or sensitivity toward new venture opportunities.	.84		
"Seeing" potential new venture opportunities does *not* come very naturally to me.	-.77		
If I recognize a good opportunity, I can raise the capital needed to take advantage of the opportunity.		.54	
Overall, I am satisfied with the growth and development of my firm.		.84	
Compared to your expectations when you first started your firm, sales have been. **		.75	
I can recognize potential new venture opportunities in industries where I have no personal experience.			.67

Table 36. (Continued)

ITEM	Factors*		
	1	2	3
The new venture opportunities I have recognized over the years have been mostly unrelated to each other.			.62
Recognizing good opportunities usually requires "immersion" in a specific industry or market place.			-.80
Eigenvalue	2.7	1.8	1.2
Alpha	.77	.56	.51
Percentage of Variance Explained	26.80	18.20	12.40

* Loadings with an absolute value of .50 were considered significant

** All responses were coded on a 5-point scale from 1=Strongly Disagree to 5=Strongly Agree (3=Neutral) except this one which was scored as shown as 2=better than expected; 1=about what I expected; 0=worse than I expected. Responses were standardized prior to being entered in this factor analysis.

Pursuers." They may be entrepreneurs who are well connected to financial capital sources or outside investors and who are, thus, well prepared to pursue opportunities. Their satisfaction with their firms may be due to the fact that they are well funded and do not have to worry about financing.

The third factor was different from the other two types in that Factor 3 entrepreneurs seem to be "Opportunity Creators." They seem to be people who move from industry to industry and who believe that they have the ability to recognize opportunities in industries which they have no prior experience, and in which they have not been "immersed." The opportunities they have recognized over the years have been unrelated to each other. Jack Goeken, who founded MCI and the FTD Florist Network, may be an example of this type of entrepreneur. For these entrepreneurs, the social network may play a significant role in the pre-organization resource gathering stage. Since these entrepreneurs do not have personal experience in the industries of some of their opportunities, they may need to consult with others in their social network, or find people who can help them marshal the resources to found their firm. Studying the success rates of such entrepreneurs as compared to those with more experience in their firms' industries remains as an important research topic.

The three types of entrepreneurs will be further studied in future analyses. The results presented here are provided only as a precursor to those future studies and as a potential starting point for opportunity recognition scale development. Chapter 11 presents concluding thoughts and future research directions.

Conclusions and Future Research Directions

In the United States and around the world, entrepreneurial businesses are seen as vital to national, regional, and local economies, and public policies are increasingly encouraging new venture creation. The entrepreneur, being the person who takes the initiative, starts from a personal belief, aspiration, or mission to found and foster a business venture. But there is a great opportunity to conduct research to more fully understand the entrepreneurship process.

Opportunity recognition is the trigger that sets the entrepreneurship process in motion. However, there is little empirical study of opportunity recognition in the entrepreneurship literature. This is surprising considering that it is one of the few variables that is truly unique to the field of entrepreneurship. Most other concepts and variables fall into other fields such as strategy, marketing, organizational behavior, economics, and psychology.

This study has focused on entrepreneurial opportunity recognition through social networks. An entrepreneur's social network expands his boundary of rationality by creating and allowing access to information. As the boundary on rationality is extended, more new venture ideas and opportunities and potential competitive advantages may be recognized, screened and assessed, and then, if appropriate, acted upon. The study of the social networks of entrepreneurs, which may include multiple webs of relations, analyzes the system of relationships in which he or she operates.

In newly-founded entrepreneurial firms, the personal and organizational dimensions of social networks converge. To date, there has been little empirical exploration of the impact of social networks on opportunity recognition. This study supports the thesis that the social networks of entrepreneurs do represent important parts of the opportunity recognition process.

This contribution to the literature utilizes social network analysis techniques to examine the opportunity recognition process. The present research extends the work of Hills et al. (1997) and Koller (1988) by providing a more thorough theoretical discussion and more refined empirical tests which show support for the importance of social networks and network characteristics to new venture opportunity recognition. The work herein sheds new light on entrepreneurship and provides new directions for research. But this study, while it finds support for a number of hypothesis related to the impacts of social networks on opportunity recognition, only begins to explain the relationship between social networks and opportunity recognition. This study has opened new veins of research and further study must be conducted. These future research areas are described in the following section.

11.1 FUTURE RESEARCH NEEDS

The largest research need is for more complete analyses and data collection of entrepreneurs' full social networks. The ego-network survey method only provided a representative picture of entrepreneurs' social networks. More intensive analyses of social networks are now required to better understand the link between social network contacts and opportunity recognition. To extend this work, the ideal study of the opportunity recognition process would involve a longitudinal study of entrepreneurs and a full network analysis.

The hypotheses in this study are theoretically independent of industry and may generalize to all profit-seeking entrepreneurs. However, there may be differences in the importance of social networks to opportunity recognition among industries. Thus, a critical step is to study other samples of entrepreneurs from other industries. IT consulting entrepreneurs exist in an industry that participates in a "networking" culture which encourages joint ventures, mergers, and alliances in the information technology community (e.g., *Business Week*, 1997). It may be that in other industries the hypothesized positive affects of social networks to opportunity recognition may be enhanced. Future research should be conducted on other samples of entrepreneurs in other industries, as well as from other sampling frames (i.e., non-D&B entrepreneurs) to test the overall generalizability of the findings.

All of the firms in this study have both survived and achieved at least a modest level of success (all firms generated at least $100,000 in annual revenues). Research is needed on the firms that failed. It is possible that there were significant differences in the use of social network contacts during the opportunity recognition process. It is also possible that the use of social networks during the opportunity recognition phase of new venture creation can reduce the liability of newness faced by newly founded firms (Stinchcombe, 1965). Again, longitudinal research would appear to be the ideal method to test this hypothesis.

Opportunity recognition is clearly a process rather than a one-time "eureka" event. Entrepreneurs indicated that opportunity recognition occurred over an extended time period (for many it was months and even years), and that changes occurred in both the new venture idea and the opportunity itself before firm founding. Future studies of opportunity recognition should attempt to better understand the specific changes to new venture ideas that occur during pre-founding activities. In addition, feedback mechanisms may be an important contribution to the basic research model in this study. Longitudinal and qualitative data should be collected to better understand the specific activities that occur and the relative importance of each activity.

Future research should also study the effects of social networks on the opportunity recognition processes of women and minority entrepreneurs. The sample in this study was mostly white male entrepreneurs. Research has shown that women and minorities develop different types of networks than their white male counterparts (Ibarra, 1992; 1993), and these differences can affect social and political attitudes (Bienenstock et al., 1990). It is possible that by oversampling women and minority entrepreneurs, we may find that social network variables have more significant impacts on opportunity recognition for minority and female entrepreneurs. Ultimately, understanding differential patterns in the social networks of entrepreneurs in traditionally disadvantaged groups may help to explain the continuing disparities in revenues as compared to their white male counterparts (e.g., Fischer et al., 1993; Kalleberg and Leicht, 1991; Sexton, 1989).

Finally, further research should determine how successful entrepreneurs develop their ties. It is likely that certain personal characteristics of entrepreneurs improve the chances for opportunity recognition by improving the ability to have and/or build networks which are conducive to recognition. However, there are also characteristics of an individual's social situation that will make the successful application of such personal abilities more or less likely, such as educational background, socio-economic class, and perhaps even certain ethnic factors. In any event, further longitudinal study to capture the dynamic processes of network development will be needed.

11.2 IMPACTS TO PUBLIC POLICY AND EDUCATIONAL PROGRAMS ON ENTREPRENEURSHIP

Public policy initiatives and educational programs should be structured to reflect these findings. Idea exchange and network-building exercises should be incorporated into training programs. More attention should also be placed on "know who" rather than "know how." From a public policy perspective, government contracts could be used as a vehicle to promote individual and interfirm cooperation by requiring team arrangements. For example, contracting officers could encourage entrepreneurs to seek out partners for bids which would help them develop their social networks. The further development of government sponsored mentoring programs in which smaller companies can be eligible for set-aside contracts when they team with larger companies (mentors) should be pursued. By opening channels of communication and assisting in network building strategies, the government may be able to improve the overall number of firms which can recognize business opportunities.

Academic teaching programs should stress the importance of developing good networking skills. A savvy network entrepreneur may be able to seek out individuals who can provide opportunities and ideas for opportunities, as well as needed resources to facilitate firm founding. University programs can promote networking sessions with local entrepreneurs and classmates/peers can help would-be entrepreneurs develop their networking skills. Such sessions can also begin dialogues that can lead to the recognition of new venture ideas and opportunities. Helping to develop partnering relationships can facilitate new venture formation. In the classroom, exercises to teach network building techniques should further enhance would-be entrepreneurs' potential to recognize opportunities for their ventures.

11.3 FINAL REMARKS

The need to understand what causes entrepreneurs to be successful is greater than ever, yet much of the existing published entrepreneurship literature still relies on post hoc analyses (Van de Ven, 1992). In this study, eighteen *a priori* hypotheses were stated and empirically tested and significant results were found to support eight hypotheses. By examining network analysis constructs, this study has improved our theoretical understanding of entrepreneurship with respect to the important process of opportunity recognition. Further, the study is an important step in the continual effort to provide direction for future entrepreneurship research.

Cited Literature

Agresti, A., and Agresti, A.: Statistical analysis of qualitative variation. In *Sociological Methodology*, ed. K. F. Schuessler, pp. 204–237. San Francisco, Jossey-Bass, 1977.

Agresti, A., and Finlay, B.: *Statistical Methods for the Social Sciences*, 2nd edition, San Francisco, Dellen Publishing Company, 1986.

Aldrich, H. E., and Herker, D.: Boundary spanning roles and organizational structure. *Academy of Management Review* 2:217–230, 1977.

Aldrich, H. E., Rosen, B., and Woodward, W.: The impact of social networks on business foundings and profit: A longitudinal study. *Frontiers in Entrepreneurship Research* 7:154–168, 1987.

Aldrich, H. E., Kalleberg, A., Marsden, P., and Cassell, J.: In pursuit of evidence: Sampling procedures for locating new businesses. *Journal of Business Venturing* 4(6):367–386, 1989.

Barnes, J.: *Social Networks*. Phillippines, Addison-Wesley, 1972.

Berger, P. L., and Luckmann, T.: *The Social Construction of Reality*. New York, Doubleday, 1967.

Bhave, M. P.: A process model of entrepreneurial venture creation. *Journal of Business Venturing* 9:223–242, 1994.

Bianchi, A.: Breaking away. *Inc.* 17(16):36–41, 1995.

Bienenstock, E., Bonacich, P., and Oliver, M.: The effect of network density and homogeneity on attitude polarization. *Social Networks* 12:153–172, 1990.

Birch, D. L.: *The Job Generation Process*. Report prepared by the MIT Program on Neighborhood and Regional Change for the Economic

Development Administration, U.S. Department of Commerce, Washington, DC, 1979.

Birch, D. L.: *Job Creation in America.* New York, Free Press, 1987.

Bird, B. J.: The operation of intentions in time: The emergence of the new venture. *Entrepreneurship Theory and Practice* 17(1):11–20, 1992.

Birley, S.: Finding the new firm. *Proceedings of the 44th Academy of Management Meetings,* Boston, MA, 1984.

Birley, S.: The role of networks in the entrepreneurial process. *Journal of Business Venturing* 1:107–117, 1985.

Blalock, H. M.: *Measurement in the Social Sciences: Theories and Strategies.* Chicago, Aldine Publishing Company, 1974.

Boissevain, J.: *Friends of Friends: Networks, Manipulators, and Coalitions.* Oxford, Blackwell, 1974.

Brenner, R.: National policy and entrepreneurship: The statesman's dilemma. *Journal of Business Venturing* 2:95–101, 1987.

Brittain, J. W., and Freeman, J. H.: Organizational proliferation and density dependent selection. In: *The Organizational Life Cycle,* eds. J. R. Kimberly and R. H. Miles, pp. 291–338. San Francisco, Jossey-Bass, 1980.

Brockhaus, R. H.: Risk taking propensity of entrepreneurs. *Academy of Management Journal* 23(3):509–520, 1980.

Brockhaus, R. H., and Horwitz, P. S.: The psychology of the entrepreneur. In: *Encyclopedia of Entrepreneurship,* eds. C. Kent, D. Sexton, and K. H. Vesper, pp. 39–57. Englewood Cliffs, NJ, Prentice Hall, 1986.

Bull, I., and Willard, G. E.: Towards a theory of entrepreneurship. *Journal of Business Venturing* 8(3):183–195, 1993.

Burt, R. S.: Network items and the general social survey. *Social Networks* 6:293–339, 1984.

Burt, R. S.: General social survey items. *Connections* 8:119–122, 1985.

Burt, R. S.: A cautionary note. *Social Networks* 8:205–211, 1986.

Burt, R. S.: A note on strangers, friends, and happiness. *Social Networks* 9:311–331, 1987.

Burt, R. S.: *Structural Holes: The Social Structure of Competition.* Cambridge, MA, Harvard University Press, 1992.

Busenitz, L.: Research on entrepreneurial alertness. *Journal of Small Business Management* 34(4):35–44, 1996.

Busenitz, L., and Murphy, G.: New evidence in the pursuit of locating new businesses. *Journal of Business Venturing* 11:221–231, 1996.

Business Week: Silicon Valley: How it really works. *Business Week,* Special Double Issue, August 18–25, 1997.

Bygrave, W.: The entrepreneurship paradigm (I): A philosophical look at its research methodologies. *Entrepreneurship Theory and Practice* 14(1):7–26, 1989a.

Bygrave, W.: The entrepreneurship paradigm (II): Chaos and catastrophes among quantum jumps. *Entrepreneurship Theory and Practice* 14(2) :7–30, 1989b.

Bygrave, B.: *The Portable MBA in Entrepreneurship.* New York, John Wiley & Sons, 1994.

Bygrave, W., and Hofer, C.: Theorizing about entrepreneurship. *Entrepreneurship Theory and Practice* 15:7–25, 1991.

Byrne, J.: The 21st century economy: How it will work. *Business Week,* August 31:104–106, 1998.

Campbell, K., Marsden, P., and Hurlbert, J.: Social resources and socioeconomic status. *Social Networks* 8:97–117, 1986.

Cameron, K. S.: Strategies for successful organizational downsizing. *Human Resource Management* 33(2):189–211, 1994.

Carland, J. W., Hoy, F., and Carland, J. C.: "Who is an entrepreneur?" is a question worth asking. *American Journal of Small Business* 13:33–39, 1988.

Carroll, G. R., and Hannan, M. T.: Density dependence in the evolution of populations of newspaper organizations. *American Sociological Review* 54:524–541, 1989.

Carter, N. M., Gartner, W. B., and Reynolds, P. D.: Exploring start-up event sequences. *Journal of Business Venturing* 11:151–166, 1996.

Case, J.: The origins of entrepreneurship. *Inc.* June: 54, 1989.

Chaganti, R., and Parasuraman, S.: A study of the impacts of gender on business performance and management patterns in small businesses. *Entrepreneurship Theory and Practice* 21(2): 73–75, 1996.

Chandler, G. N. and Hanks, S. H.: Market attractiveness, resource-based capabilities, venture strategies, and venture performance. *Journal of Business Venturing* 9(4):331–349, 1994.

Child, D.: *The Essentials of Factor Analysis.* 2nd. edition, London, Cassell Educational Ltd., 1990.

Christensen, P. S., Madsen, O. O., and Peterson, R.: *Opportunity Identification: The Contribution of Entrepreneurship to Strategic Management.* Denmark, Aarhus University Institute of Management, 1989.

Christensen, P. S., Madsen, O. O., and Peterson, R.: Conceptualizing entrepreneurial opportunity recognition. In: *Marketing and*

Entrepreneurship: Research Ideas and Opportunities, ed. G. E. Hills, pp. 61–75. Westport, CT, Quorum Books, 1994.

Christensen, P. S., and Peterson, R.: Opportunity identification: Mapping the sources of new venture ideas. Paper presented at the *10th Annual Babson Entrepreneurship Research Conference,* April. Denmark, Aarhus University Institute of Management, 1990.

Cohen, J., and Cohen, P.: *Applied Multiple Regression/Correlation Analysis for the Behavioral Sciences.* Hillsdale, NJ, Lawrence Erlbaum Associates, 1975.

Collins, J. C., and Lazier, W. C.: *Beyond Entrepreneurship: Turning your Business into an Enduring Great Company.* Englewood Cliffs, NJ, Prentice Hall, 1992.

Cooper, A. C., Dunkelberg, W., Woo, C., and Dennis, W.: *New Business in America: The Firms and their Owners.* Washington, DC, The National Federation of Independent Business, 1990.

Covin, J., and Slevin, D.: A conceptual model of entrepreneurship as a firm behavior. *Entrepreneurship Theory and Practice* 16(1): 7–25, 1991.

Cyert, R. M., and March, J. G.: *A Behavioral Theory of the Firm.* Englewood Cliffs, NJ, Prentice Hall, 1963.

D&B: *D&B Census of American Business.* Bethlehem, PA, Dun & Bradstreet Corporation, 1997a.

D&B: *D&B Million Dollar Directory.* Bethlehem, PA, Dun & Bradstreet Corporation, 1997b.

d'Amboise G., and Muldowney, M.: Management theory for small business: Attempts and requirements. *Academy of Management Review* 13:226–240, 1988.

Davern, M.: Social networks and economic sociology: A proposed research agenda for a more complete social science. *American Journal of Economics and Sociology* 56(3):287–302, 1997.

Dennis, W. J., Phillips, B. D., and Starr, E.: Small business job creation: The findings and their critics. *Business Economics* 29(3): 23–30, 1994.

Drucker, P. F.: *Innovation and Entrepreneurship: Practice and Principles.* New York, Harper & Row, 1985.

Dubini, P., and Aldrich, H.: Personal and extended networks are central to the entrepreneurship process. *Journal of Business Venturing* 6(5):305–313, 1991.

Dyer, W. G.: *The Entrepreneurial Experience.* San Francisco, CA: Jossey-Bass, 1992.

Fichman, M., and Levinthal, D. A.: Honeymoons and the liability of adolescence: A new perspective on duration dependence in social and organizational relationships. *Academy of Management Review* 16:442–468, 1991.

Fabowale, L, Orser, B., and Riding, A.: Gender, structural factors, and credit terms between Canadian small businesses and financial institutions. *Entrepreneurship Theory and Practice* 19(4): 41–65, 1995.

Fischer, E, Reuber, A., and Dyke, L.: A theoretical overview of research on sex, gender, and entrepreneurship. *Journal of Business Venturing* 8:151–168, 1993.

Gaglio, C. M., and Taub, R. P.: Entrepreneurs and opportunity recognition. *Frontiers of Entrepreneurship Research* 12:136–147, 1992.

Gartner, W. B.: A conceptual framework for describing the phenomenon of new venture creation. *Academy of Management Review* 10(4):696–706, 1985.

Gartner, W. B.: "Who is an entrepreneur?" is the wrong question. *American Journal of Small Business* 13:11–32, 1988.

Gartner, W. B.: Some suggestions for research on entrepreneurial traits and characteristics. *Entrepreneurship Theory and Practice* 14(1):27–37, 1989.

Gartner, W. B.: What are we talking about when we talk about entrepreneurship? *Journal of Business Venturing* 5:15–28, 1990.

Gartner, W. B., Bird, B., and Starr, J.: Acting as if: Differentiating entrepreneurial from organizational behavior. *Entrepreneurship Theory and Practice* 16(3):13–31, 1992.

Gilad, B., Kaish, S., and Ronen, J.: Information, search and entrepreneurship: A pilot study. *Journal of Behavioral Economics* 18:217–235, 1989.

Granovetter, M.: The strength of weak ties. *American Journal of Sociology* 78(6):1360–1380, 1973.

Granovetter, M.: The strength of weak ties: A network theory revisited. In: *Social Structure and Network Analysis,* eds. P. V. Marsden and N. Lin, pp. 105–130. Beverly Hills, Sage, 1982.

Granovetter, M.: Economic action and social structure: A theory of embeddedness. *American Journal of Sociology* 91(3):481–510, 1985.

Granovetter, M.: Problems of explanation in economic sociology. In: *Networks and Organizations,* eds. N. Nohria and R. G. Eccles, pp. 25–56. Boston, MA, Harvard Business School Press, 1994.

Gupta, U.: New business incorporation reached record in 1994. *Wall Street Journal,* June 6:B2, 1995.

Hambrick, D. C., and Lei, D.: Toward an empirical prioritization of contingency variables for business strategy. *Academy of Management Journal* 28:763–788, 1985.

Hammer, M., and Champy, J.: *Reengineering the Corporation: A Manifesto for Business Revolution.* Chapter 5, New York, HarperCollins, 1993.

Hannan, M. T., and Freeman, J.: The population ecology of organizations. *American Journal of Sociology* 82:929–964, 1977.

Hansen, E. L.: Entrepreneurial networks and new organization growth. *Entrepreneurship Theory and Practice* 19(4):7–19, 1995.

Hansen, E. L., and Allen, K. R.: The creation corridor: Environmental load and Pre-organization information-processing ability. *Entrepreneurship Theory and Practice* 17(1):57–66, 1992.

Haung, G. and Tausig, M.: Network range in personal networks. *Social Networks* 12:261–268, 1990.

Herron, L., and Sapienza, H. J.: The entrepreneur and the initiation of new venture launch activities. *Entrepreneurship Theory and Practice* 17(1):49–56, 1992.

Hills, G. E.: *Marketing and Entrepreneurship: Research Ideas and Opportunities.* Westport, CT, Quorum Books, 1994.

Hills, G. E.: Opportunity recognition by successful entrepreneurs: A pilot study. *Frontiers of Entrepreneurship Research* 15:105–117, 1995.

Hills, G. E.: Opportunity recognition: Perceptions and behaviors of entrepreneurs. Research Report submitted to the E. M. Kauffman Foundation, Kansas City, 1996.

Hills, G. E., Lumpkin, G. T., and Singh, R.: Opportunity recognition: Perceptions and behaviors of entrepreneurs. *Frontiers of Entrepreneurship Research* 17:168–182, 1997.

Hof, R. D.: E-commerce: The net is open for business—big time. *Business Week* August 31:108–109, 1998.

Hofer, C. W.: Toward a contingency theory of business strategy. *Academy of Management Journal* 18:784–810, 1975.

Hogan, B.: How to hatch new businesses. *D&B Reports* 39(4):54–55, 1991.

Ibarra, H.: Homophily and differential returns: Sex differences in network structure and access in an advertising firm. *Administrative Science Quarterly* 37:422–447, 1992.

Ibarra, H.: Personal networks of women and minorities in management: A conceptual framework. *Academy of Management Review* 18:56–87, 1993.

IES: Nomination/application for John Goeken for consideration of induction into the Chicago Area Entrepreneurship Hall of Fame.

Submitted to the University of Illinois at Chicago Institute for Entrepreneurial Studies (IES), 1992.

IES: Nomination/application for Barry Potekin for consideration of induction into the Chicago Area Entrepreneurship Hall of Fame. Submitted to the University of Illinois at Chicago Institute for Entrepreneurial Studies (IES), 1994.

IES: Nomination/application for Shari Whitley for consideration of induction into the Chicago Area Entrepreneurship Hall of Fame. Submitted to the University of Illinois at Chicago Institute for Entrepreneurial Studies (IES), 1996.

Johannisson, B.: Anarchists and organizers: Entrepreneurs in a network perspective. *International Studies of Management and Organization* 17(1):49–63, 1987.

Johannisson, B.: Economics of overview - guiding the external growth of small firms. *International Small Business Journal* 9:32– 44, 1990.

Kaish, S., and Gilad, B.: Characteristics of opportunity search for entrepreneurs versus executives: Sources, interests, general alertness. *Journal of Business Venturing* 6(1):45–61, 1991.

Kalleberg, A. L., and Leicht, K. T.: Gender and organizational performance: Determinants of small business survival and success. *Academy of Management Journal* 34(1):136–161, 1991.

Kanter, R. M.: Some effects of proportions on group life: Skewed sex ratios and responses to token women. *American Journal of Sociology* 82:965–990, 1977.

Karagozoglu, N., and Lindell, M.: Internationalization of small and medium-sized technology-based firms: An exploratory study. *Journal of Small Business Management* 36(1):44–59, 1998.

Katz, J., and Gartner, W. B.: Properties of emerging organizations. *Academy of Management Review* 13(3):429–441, 1988.

Kim, J., and Mueller, C. W.: *Introduction to Factor Analysis: What it is and how to do it.* Newbury Park, Sage Publications, 1978.

Kirchoff, B. A.: Entrepreneurship's contribution to economics. *Entrepreneurship Theory and Practice* 16(2):93–112, 1991.

Kirchoff, B. A., and Greene, P. G.: Response to renewed attacks on the small business job creation hypothesis. *Frontiers of Entrepreneurship Research* 15:1–13, 1995.

Kirchoff, B. A., and McAuliffe, R. E.: *Economic Redevelopment of Mature Industrial Areas.* A report prepared for the Economic Development Administration, U.S. Department of Commerce, 1989.

Kirchoff, B. A., and Phillips, B. D.: Research applications of the small business data base of the U.S. Small Business Administration. In: *The State of the Art of Entrepreneurship,* eds. D. L. Sexton and J. D. Kasarda, pp. 243–267. Boston, MA, PWS-Kent Publishing Company, 1992.

Kirzner, I. M.: *Competition and Entrepreneurship.* Chicago, IL, University of Chicago Press, 1973.

Kirzner, I. M.: *Perception, Opportunity, and Profit: Studies in the Theory of Entrepreneurship.* Chicago, IL, University of Chicago Press, 1979.

Koller, R. H.: On the source of entrepreneurial ideas. *Frontiers of Entrepreneurship Research* 8:194–207, 1988.

Kotler, P.: *Marketing Management: Analysis, Planning, Implementation, and Control.* 7th edition, Englewood Cliffs, NJ, Prentice-Hall, Inc., 1991.

Lambkin, M.: Order of entry and performance in new markets. *Strategic Management Journal* 9:127–140, 1988.

Larson, A., and Starr, J. A.: A network model of organization formation. *Entrepreneurship Theory and Practice* 17(2):5–15, 1993.

Laumann, E. O., Galskeiwicz, L., and Marsden, P. V.: Community structure as interorganizational linkages. *Annual Review of Sociology* 4:455–484, 1978.

Lawless, M., and Anderson, P.: Generational technological change: Effects of innovation and local rivalry on performance. *Academy of Management Journal* 39:1185–1217, 1996.

Lawrence, P. R., and Lorsch, J. W.: *Organization and Environment: Managing Differentiation and Integration.* Boston, MA, Graduate School of Business Administration, Harvard University, 1967.

Learned, K. E.: What happened before the organization? A model of organization formation. *Entrepreneurship Theory and Practice* 17(1):39–48, 1992.

Long, W., and McMullan, W. E.: Mapping the new venture opportunity identification process. *Frontiers of Entrepreneurship Research* 4:567–590, 1984.

Low, M. B., and MacMillan, I. C.: Entrepreneurship: Past research and future challenges, *Journal of Management* 14:139–161, 1988.

Lumpkin, G. T., and Dess, G. G.: Clarifying the entrepreneurial orientation construct and linking it to performance. *Academy of Management Review* 21:135–172, 1996.

Marsden, P.: Core discussion networks of Americans. *American Sociological Review* 52: 122–131, 1987.

Marsden, P.: Network data and measurement. *Annual Review of Sociology* 16:435–463, 1990.

Masten, J., Hartmann, G. B., and Safari, A.: Small business strategic planning and technology transfer: The use of publicly supported technology assistance. *Journal of Small Business Management* 33(3):26–37, 1995.

Mayhew, B. H., and Levinger, R. L.: Size and the density of interaction in human aggregates. *American Journal of Sociology* 82: 86–110, 1976.

McClelland, D. C.: *The Achieving Society.* Princeton, NJ, D. Van Nostrand Company, Inc., 1961.

McMullan, W. E., and Long, W. A.: *Developing New Ventures: The Entrepreneurial Option.* San Diego, CA, Harcourt Brace Jovanovich, 1990.

Mehra, A., Kilduff, M., and Brass, D. J.: At the margins: A distinctiveness approach to the social identity and social networks of underrepresented groups. *Academy of Management Journal* 41(4): 441–452, 1998.

Merriam-Webster Dictionary: *The New Merriam-Webster Dictionary.* Springfield, MA, Merriam-Webster Publishers, 1989.

Merz, G. R., Weber, P. B., and Laetz, V. B.: Linking small business management with entrepreneurial growth. *Journal of Small Business Management* 32(4):48–60, 1994.

Meyer, J. W., and Rowan, B.: Institutionalized organizations: Formal structure as myth and ceremony. *American Journal of Sociology* 83:340–363, 1977.

Mitchell, J.: The concept and use of social networks. In: *Social Networks in Urban Situations,* ed. J. Mitchell, pp. 1–50. Manchester, Manchester University Press, 1969.

Nohria, N.: Information search in the creation of new business ventures: The case of the 128 venture group. In: *Networks and Organizations: Structure, Form, and Action,* eds. N. Nohria and R. Eccles, pp. 240–261. Boston, MA, Harvard Business School Press, 1992.

Norusis, M. J.: *The SPSS Guide to Data Analysis for SPSS/PC+.* 2nd edition, Chicago, IL, SPSS, Inc, 1991.

Ozanne, U. B., and Hunt, S. D.: *The Economics of Franchising.* Issued as a committee print for the Select Committee on Small Business, U.S. Senate, 92nd Congress, 1st Session, Washington DC, 1971.

Phan, P. H., Butler, J. E., and Lee, S. H.: Crossing mother: Entrepreneur-franchisees' attempts to reduce franchisor influence. *Journal of Business Venturing* 11(5):379–402, 1996.

Pool, I., and Kochen, M.: Contacts and influence. *Social Networks* 1:5–51, 1978.

Porter, M. E.: How competitive forces shape strategy. *Harvard Business Review* 57,(2):137–145, 1979.

Powell, W. W.: Neither market nor hierarchy: Network forms or organization. *Research in Organizational Behavior* 12:295–336, 1990.

Powell, W. W., and DiMaggio, P.: *The New Institutionalism in Organizational Analysis.* Chicago, University of Chicago Press, 1991.

Reinhardt, A.: Risks and rewards: No slacking in Silicon Valley. *Business Week* August 31: 88–92, 1998.

Reynolds, P. D.: Sociology and entrepreneurship: Concepts and contributions. *Entrepreneurship Theory and Practice* 16(2):47–70, 1992.

Reynolds, P. D.: Rescuing barriers to understanding new firm gestation: Prevalence and success of nascent entrepreneurs. Paper presented at the *Academy of Management Meetings,* Dallas, TX, August, 1994.

Romanelli, E.: Environments and strategies of organization start-up: Effects on early survival. *Administrative Science Quarterly* 34:369–387, 1989.

Ronstadt, R.: The corridor principle. *Journal of Business Venturing* 3:31–40, 1988.

Rotter, J. B.: Generalized expectancies for internal versus external control of reinforcement. *Psychological Monographs: General and Applied* 80(1):1–28, 1966.

Sandberg, W. R.: *New Venture Performance: The Role of Strategy and Industry Structure.* Lexington, MA, Lexington Books, 1986.

Schumpeter, J.: *The Theory of Economic Development.* Cambridge, MA, Harvard University Press, 1934.

Seppa, N.: Downsizing: A new form of abandonment. *APA Monitor* 26(5):1, 1996.

Serwer, A. E.: Layoffs tail off—but only for some. *Fortune* March 20:14, 1995.

Sexton, D.: Research on women owned businesses: Current status and future predictions. In: *Women Owned Businesses,* eds. O. Hagan, C. Rivchun, and D. Sexton, pp. 183–194. New York, Praeger, 1989.

Sexton, D., and Bowman, N. B.: Comparative entrepreneurship: Characteristics of students. *Frontiers in Entrepreneurship Research* 4:513–529, 1984.

Shane, S.: Explaining variation in rates of entrepreneurship in the United States: 1899–1988. *Journal of Management* 22(5):747–781, 1996.

Shane, S.: Presentation/Discussion by Scott Shane about theory development in entrepreneurship at the *1997 Babson College-Kauffman Foundation Research Conference* Babson College, Massachusetts, April 16, 1997.

Shapero, A. and Giglierano, J.: Exits and entries: A study in yellow pages journalism. *Frontiers in Entrepreneurship Research* 2:113– 141, 1982.

Simon, H. A.: *Administrative Behavior.* 3rd edition, New York, Free Press, 1976.

Singh, J. V., Tucker, D. J., and House, R. J.: Organizational change and organizational mortality. *Administrative Science Quarterly* 31:587–611, 1986.

Singh, R., Hybels, R., Ouksel, A., and Ahmed, I.: Technology diffusion through the social networks of entrepreneurs: Evidence of differences among demographic groups. Working Paper, University of Illinois at Chicago, Chicago, 1997.

Smeltzer, L., Fann, G., and Nikolesean, N.: Environmental scanning practices in small business. *Journal of Small Business Management* 26(3):55–62, 1988.

Stasch, S.: Identifying new venture ideas: What we know and don't know. In: *Research at the Marketing/Entrepreneurship Interface,* eds. G. E. Hills, R. W. LaForge, and B. J. Parker, pp. 325–330. Chicago, University of Illinois at Chicago, 1990.

Stearns, T., and Hills, G. E.: Entrepreneurship and new firm development: A definitional introduction. *Journal of Business Research* 36:1–4, 1996.

Stevenson, H. H., and Gumpert, D. E.: The heart of entrepreneurship. *Harvard Business Review* 63(2):85–94, 1985.

Stevenson, H. H., and Jarillo-Mossi, J. C.: Preserving entrepreneurship as companies grow. *Journal of Business Strategy* 7:10–23, 1986.

Stevenson, H. H., Roberts, M. J., and Grousbeck, H. I.: *New Business Ventures and the Entrepreneur.* 3rd edition, Homewood, IL, Richard D. Irwin, Inc., 1989.

Stinchcombe, A. L. (1965). Social structure in organizations. In J. G. March (Ed.), *Handbook of organizations:* 142–193. Chicago, Rand McNally, 1965.

Stinchcombe, A. L.: *Information and Organizations.* Berkeley, CA, University of California Press, 1990.

Stuart, R. W., and Abetti, P. A.: Impact of entrepreneurial and management experience on early performance. *Journal of Business Venturing* 5:151–162, 1990.

Teach, R. D., Schwartz, R. G., and Tarpley, F. A.: The recognition and exploitation of opportunity in the software industry: A study of surviving firms. *Frontiers of Entrepreneurship Research* 9:383–397, 1989.

Thompson, A. A. and Strickland, A. J.: *Strategic Management: Concepts and Cases.* 6th edition, Homewood, IL, Irwin, 1992.

Timmons, J. A.: Growing up big. In: *The Art and Science of Entrepreneurship,* eds. C Sexton, D. L., and Smilor, R. W., pp. 223–239. Cambridge, MA, Ballinger, 1986.

Timmons, J. A.: *New Business Opportunities: Getting to the Right Place at the Right Time.* Acton, MA: Brick House Publishing Co., 1990.

Timmons, J. A.: *New Venture Creation: Entrepreneurship for the 21st Century.* 4th edition, Burr Ridge, IL, Irwin, 1994a.

Timmons, J. A.: Opportunity recognition: The search for higher-potential ventures. In: *The Portable MBA in Entrepreneurship,* ed. W. D. Bygrave, pp. 26–54. New York, John Wiley & Sons, 1994b.

Timmons, J. A., Muzyka, D. F., Stevenson, H. H., and Bygrave, W. D.: Opportunity recognition: The core of entrepreneurship. *Frontiers of Entrepreneurship Research* 7:109–123, 1987.

Timmons, J. A., and Muzyka, D. F.: Opportunity recognition: Lessons from venture capital. In: *Marketing and Entrepreneurship: Research Ideas and Opportunities,* ed. G. E. Hills, pp. 95–114. Westport, Connecticut, Quorum Books, 1994.

Tjosvold, D., and Weicker, D.: Cooperative and competitive networking by entrepreneurs: A critical incident study. *Journal of Small Business Management* 31(1):11–21, 1993.

Tsui, A. S., Egan, T. D., and O'Reilly, C. A.: Being different: Relational demography and organizational attachment. *Administrative Science Quarterly* 37:549–579, 1992.

Tushman, M. L., and Anderson, P.: Technological discontinuities and organizational environments. *Administrative Science Quarterly* 31:439–465, 1986.

Utterback, J. M., and Suárez, F. F.: Innovation, competition, and industry structure. *Research Policy* 22:1–61, 1993.

Uzzi, B.: The sources and consequences of embeddedness for the economic performance of organizations: The network effect. *American Sociological Review* 61(4):674–698, 1996.

Van de Ven, A. H.: Longitudinal methods for studying the process of entrepreneurship. In: *The State of the Art of Entrepreneurship*, eds. D. Sexton and J. Kasarda, pp. 214–242. Boston, MA, PWS-Kent Publishing Co., 1992

Van de Ven, A. H., Hudsen, R., and Schroeder, D. M.: Designing new business startups: Entrepreneurial, organizational, and ecological considerations. *Journal of Management* 10(1):87–107, 1984.

Vesper, K.: *New Venture Strategies*. Englewood Cliffs, NJ, Prentice Hall, 1980.

Vesper, K.: *New Venture Mechanics*. Englewood Cliffs, NJ, Prentice Hall, 1993.

Vesper, K.: *New Venture Experience*. Revised, Seattle, WA, Vector Books, 1996.

Wasserman, S. and Faust, K.: *Social Network Analysis: Methods and Applications*. New York, Cambridge University Press, 1994.

Webster's Dictionary: *Webster's II New Riverside Dictionary*. New York, Berkeley Books, 1984.

Wellman, B.: Structural analysis: From method and metaphor to theory and substance. In: *Social Structures: A Network Approach*, eds. B. Wellman and S. D. Berkowitz, pp. 19–61. New York, Cambridge, 1988.

Wellman, B.: An egocentric network tale. *Social Networks* 15:423–436, 1993.

White, S., and Reynolds, P. D.: Factors inhibiting ethnic participation in entrepreneurial processes. *Frontiers of Entrepreneurship Research* 17:258–259, 1997.

Williamson, O. E.: Transaction-cost economics: The governance of contractual relations. *Journal of Law and Economics* 22(2):233–261, 1979.

Zelade, R.: Global consulting grows. *International Business* 9(8):6, 1996.

Zhao, L., and Aram, J. D.: Networking and growth of young technology-intensive ventures in China. *Journal of Business Venturing* 10:349–370, 1995.

Mail Survey Questionnaire

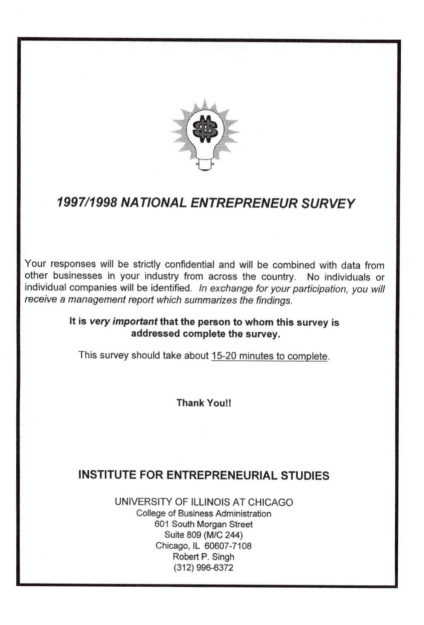

1997/1998 NATIONAL ENTREPRENEUR SURVEY

Your responses will be strictly confidential and will be combined with data from other businesses in your industry from across the country. No individuals or individual companies will be identified. *In exchange for your participation, you will receive a management report which summarizes the findings.*

It is *very important* that the person to whom this survey is addressed complete the survey.

This survey should take about 15-20 minutes to complete.

Thank You!!

INSTITUTE FOR ENTREPRENEURIAL STUDIES

UNIVERSITY OF ILLINOIS AT CHICAGO
College of Business Administration
601 South Morgan Street
Suite 809 (M/C 244)
Chicago, IL 60607-7108
Robert P. Singh
(312) 996-6372

Please keep the following in mind as you consider *ideas* and *opportunities*.

Initial New Venture Ideas → Potential New Venture Opportunities → Decision to Start a New Venture

Some people come up with initial new venture ideas. After some additional thought and/or evaluation, they may recognize that their ideas are potential new venture opportunities. With even further thought and consideration one may then decide to start a new venture.

Based on the model and brief discussion above, please answer the following questions:

A. When someone first thinks of a possible new venture, but has not evaluated it much at all, this survey would call it a "new venture _____."

    ___ idea   ___ opportunity   ___ not clearly either of these

B. When someone has given a possible new venture some additional thought and/or evaluation, this survey would say that it may lead to a "new venture _____."

    ___ idea   ___ opportunity   ___ not clearly either of these

C. Do you agree that the steps in the model illustrated above *generally* occur as shown?

    ___ yes   ___ no   ___ not sure

---

1. How/Where did you first get the initial idea for your current business? (Check all that apply)

    ___ prior experience   ___ saw a similar business
    ___ from business associates   ___ hobby/personal interest
    ___ from friends or relatives   ___ magazine or newspaper
    ___ conducted market research   ___ radio or television
    ___ It just came to mind
    ___ Other (please describe) _____

2. What activities, if any, did you do to help you recognize that your venture idea was a potential opportunity for your current firm? (Check all that apply)

    ___ None, I knew my business idea was an opportunity
    ___ Prepared financial estimates
    ___ Gathered information on competitors
    ___ Contacted potential customers/clients
    ___ Sought out information/feedback from business associates
    ___ Discussed the idea with friends and family members
    ___ Other (please describe) _____

3. Which of the following most accurately describes how you founded your firm? (Please select only one.)

    ___ I first decided to start a business. I then conducted a search for opportunities which led to my firm.
    ___ I first recognized an opportunity for my business. I then started my business to take advantage of it.

4. Approximately how much time passed between when you first had the initial idea for your current business and when you <u>recognized it was a potential opportunity</u> for a new venture? (Please check only one)

  ___ none   ___ hours   ___ days   ___ weeks   ___ months   ___ years

5. Approximately how much time passed between when you first recognized the potential opportunity for your current business and when you <u>actually started</u> your business? (Please check only one)

  ___ hours   ___ days   ___ weeks   ___ months   ___ years

6. How much did you modify your initial venture idea before it became the potential opportunity for your current business?

  ___No Change   ___Slight Change   ___Moderate Change   ___Major Change   ___Completely Changed

7. How much did you modify your initial venture idea before you actually started your business?

  ___No Change   ___Slight Change   ___Moderate Change   ___Major Change   ___Completely Changed

8. How many people did you *discuss* your potential venture opportunity with prior to founding your current firm?

  ___ 0   ___ 1-2   ___ 3-4   ___ 5-6   ___ 7-8   ___ 9-10   ___ 11+

  8a. If you did discuss your potential venture opportunity with others prior to founding, how much did you modify your initial venture idea based on these discussions?

  ___No Change   ___Slight Change   ___Moderate Change   ___Major Change   ___Completely Changed

9. In order to identify new venture opportunities, how often do you hold meetings with your employees?

  ___ Never   ___ Daily   ___ Weekly   ___ Monthly   ___ Quarterly   ___ Annually   ___ As Needed

Please check only one box for each question.

Question	0	1	2	3	4	5	6	7	8-10	11+
10. Last <u>month</u>, how many venture *ideas* did you have that could lead to potential new venture opportunities?										
11. Last <u>year</u>, how many venture *ideas* did you have that could lead to potential new venture opportunities?										
12. Based on the ideas you had last <u>month</u>, how many potential new venture *opportunities* did you recognize?										
13. Based on the ideas you had last <u>year</u>, how many potential new venture *opportunities* did you recognize?										
14. How many of the opportunities you recognized in the last <u>year</u> were unrelated to your current business?										
15. In the last <u>year</u>, how many new venture opportunities did you *pursue* (invested time and money)?										
16. How many of the opportunities you pursued (in the prior question) do you consider to be successes?										

This section asks how you learned about opportunities. **We do *not* ask for any confidential information.**

17. Think back to when you first recognized the opportunity for your firm. Please list the 5 people from whom you received information that *led you to recognize potential new venture opportunities* since that time (including the opportunity for your firm). These people may include friends, family, employees, business associates, co-workers, professors, and others who may be inside or outside your firm. If there are less than five, answer for as many as appropriate. If there is no one, please go to Question 26.

Helped you recognize the opportunity for your current firm? (Please circle one)

A) _____   Yes / No

B) _____   Yes / No   ***Use initials or first names***

C) _____   Yes / No

D) _____   Yes / No   **Please keep this list in mind as you complete the rest of this section.**

E) _____   Yes / No

18. How many others provided you with information about new venture opportunities (if any)? _____

19. These questions ask how well each pair of people on your list know each other, *to the best of your knowledge*. **Circle the best answer for each.**

Person A and Person B know each other:	Not at All	/ Some /	Very Well
Person A and Person C know each other:	Not at All	/ Some /	Very Well
Person A and Person D know each other:	Not at All	/ Some /	Very Well
Person A and Person E know each other:	Not at All	/ Some /	Very Well
Person B and Person C know each other:	Not at All	/ Some /	Very Well
Person B and Person D know each other:	Not at All	/ Some /	Very Well
Person B and Person E know each other:	Not at All	/ Some /	Very Well
Person C and Person D know each other:	Not at All	/ Some /	Very Well
Person C and Person E know each other:	Not at All	/ Some /	Very Well
Person D and Person E know each other:	Not at All	/ Some /	Very Well

20. Which of the following would best describe each person on your list? (Circle one for each person)

Latino American	A	B	C	D	E
African American	A	B	C	D	E
Native American	A	B	C	D	E
Asian American (not Indian)	A	B	C	D	E
Indian (not Native American)	A	B	C	D	E
White	A	B	C	D	E

21. Which of the following people on your list are male and female? (Circle one for each person)

male	A	B	C	D	E
female	A	B	C	D	E

22. How well do you personally know each of the people you have identified? (Circle one for each person)

very well	A	B	C	D	E
fairly well	A	B	C	D	E
somewhat	A	B	C	D	E
not very well	A	B	C	D	E

23. Which persons on your list are: (It is OK to circle more than one for each person)

co-founders?	A	B	C	D	E
current employees of your firm?	A	B	C	D	E
former co-workers?	A	B	C	D	E
relatives of yours?	A	B	C	D	E
personal friends of yours?	A	B	C	D	E
customers of your firm?	A	B	C	D	E
suppliers to your firm?	A	B	C	D	E
business associates?	A	B	C	D	E
other business owners?	A	B	C	D	E

24. As far as you know, which of the people on your list has: (Circle only the highest level of education attained by each person)

A graduate degree?	A	B	C	D	E
Some grad. education, but no grad. degree?	A	B	C	D	E
A bachelor's degree?	A	B	C	D	E
Some college education, but no bachelor's?	A	B	C	D	E
A high school degree?	A	B	C	D	E
some high school education, but no degree?	A	B	C	D	E

25. Based on your best guess, which persons on your list are: (Circle one for each person)

60 or older?	A	B	C	D	E
between 50 and 59?	A	B	C	D	E
between 40 and 49?	A	B	C	D	E
between 30 and 39?	A	B	C	D	E
younger than 30?	A	B	C	D	E

Based on your experience, please respond to the following *(check only one box for each question)*

Question	Strongly Agree	Agree	Neutral	Disagree	Strongly Disagree
26. Sometimes I feel I don't have enough control over the direction my life is taking.					
27. Success is a matter of hard work; luck has little or nothing to do with it.					
28. I would never have started my business, if I knew then what I now know.					
29. While going about routine day-to-day activities, I see potential new venture ideas all around me.					
30. I often do financial calculations in my head when I see potential new venture ideas.					
31. I have a special "alertness" or sensitivity toward new venture opportunities.					
32. Recognizing opportunities is really several learning steps over time, rather than a "eureka" experience.					
33. It is easier to see opportunities after you start a business and enter the market (as compared to before you start).					
34. I can recognize potential new venture opportunities in industries where I have no personal experience.					
35. Having the money to take advantage of an opportunity has little to do with *recognizing* an opportunity.					
36. New venture ideas are a dime a dozen. Evaluation is the key to recognizing *good* opportunities.					
37. Conducting formal market analyses is important to recognizing new venture opportunities.					
38. Social contacts (friends, family, business contacts, etc.) are important to recognizing opportunities.					
39. The new venture opportunities I have recognized over the years have been mostly unrelated to each other.					
40. "Seeing" potential new venture opportunities does not come very naturally to me.					
41. Recognizing good opportunities usually requires "immersion" in a specific industry or marketplace.					
42. If I recognize a good opportunity, I can raise the capital needed to take advantage of the opportunity.					
43. "Gut feel" is important to recognizing opportunities.					
44. Overall, I am satisfied with the growth and development of my firm.					

45. Are you one of the founders of your current firm? (Please circle one)   YES / NO
    45a. If YES, how many other co-founders were there (if any)?   0   1   2   3   4 or more
    45b. How many years of experience in your industry did you have prior to starting your firm? _____
    45c. What year did you start your business? 19_____

46. Since your firm was founded, have you started any major, new part of your business?   YES / NO
    46a. If YES, about what % of your total sales volume is it (or are they) today? _____%

47. Including your current firm, how many businesses have you founded or co-founded? _____
    47a. How many different industries have you founded businesses in?   1   2   3   4 or more

48. Are you a franchisee?   YES / NO

49. Compared to your expectations when you first started your firm, sales have been:
    ___ better than I expected   ___ about what I expected   ___ worse than I expected

Please answer the following questions describing yourself. Your responses to these questions will NOT be released to anyone on an individual basis. They will only be used to describe the characteristics of all individuals responding to the survey.

50. Are you male or female?   MALE / FEMALE

51. What is your age? _____ (years)

52. Of the following, which best describes you? (Please check one)
    _____ Latino American   _____ Asian American (not Indian)
    _____ African American   _____ Indian American (not Native American)
    _____ White American   _____ Native American
    _____ Other (please specify _____)

53. Did you immigrate to the USA?   YES / NO
    53a. If YES, how many years ago? _____

54. What is your highest level of formal education? (Please check one)
    _____ Some high school education, but no diploma
    _____ High school degree
    _____ Some college education, but no Bachelor's degree
    _____ Bachelor's degree
    _____ Some graduate education, but no graduate degree
    _____ Graduate degree
    54a. College Major(s) (if any): _____

END OF SURVEY - Thank you for your time and cooperation!

Cover Letters and Postcard Reminder Wording

November 10, 1997

Entrepreneur Name
Company Name
Address
City, State Zip

Dear _____:

We need your assistance! The nationally ranked Institute for Entrepreneurial Studies at the University of Illinois at Chicago (UIC) is conducting this study to gain a better understanding of entrepreneurship and to improve the quality of entrepreneurship education. We would greatly appreciate it if you would take the time to answer the questions in the enclosed survey and return it in the postage paid envelope. We assure you that your responses will be held in **strict confidence** and that the survey results will be presented in a manner that will protect the identity of all individuals and companies.

You have been selected as part of a scientifically structured sample of information technology firms from across the country; therefore, your reply to the enclosed questionnaire is vital to the success of this study. Because of the nature of the survey, it is also important that you **complete the questionnaire yourself**.

We recognize that you are quite busy and that your time is valuable. In return for your donation of the 15-20 minutes to complete this questionnaire, we will send you a Management Summary of the survey results. You may find the information on firms in your industry valuable for strategic planning purposes.

On a personal note, I would like to appeal to **your good will and generosity** because this research is part of my Ph.D. thesis. *The overall response rate will have an impact on whether I graduate or not.* Please return the completed questionnaire as soon as possible. Should you have any questions, feel free to contact me by phone at (312) 996-6372. Thank you for your time and generous assistance in advance!

Sincerely,

Robert Singh, Research Assistant
UIC Institute for Entrepreneurial Studies

Enclosures

January 14, 1998

Entrepreneur Name
Company Name
Address
City, State Zip

Dear _____ :

Happy New Year! I hope you had a wonderful holiday season. A few weeks ago you should have received a copy of a survey in the mail as part of a national study being conducted by the Institute for Entrepreneurial Studies (IES) at the University of Illinois at Chicago. We have not received your response yet and have enclosed another copy of the survey.

IES is a **top 25 academic center** in the area of entrepreneurship. We have received numerous awards for our teaching and research efforts. Because the number of information technology firms is exploding, we want to find out more about how these firms are being started and who is starting them. You have been selected as part of a scientifically structured sample of information technology entrepreneurs from across the country; therefore, your reply to the enclosed questionnaire is vital to the success of the study.

Let me assure you that we take **great security precautions** to ensure that your response will only be used for teaching and research purposes. No individual information will ever be released. The only people who will have access to the data are Dr. Gerald Hills who is the Executive Director of IES and a world-renown expert on entrepreneurship, and me.

We recognize that you are quite busy and that your time is valuable. In return for your donation of the 15-20 minutes to complete this questionnaire, we will send you a Management Summary of the survey results. Since all of the firms in the study are information technology firms like yours, you may find the Management Summary valuable for strategic planning purposes.

I do hope you will participate in the study. Every response is critical to the better understanding of entrepreneurship and new firm creation, and will truly further our ability to teach entrepreneurship in the classroom. In addition, the more responses we receive, the sooner I graduate ☺ . If you have any questions, please feel free to send me an email at "rsingh2@uic.edu". Once again, I thank you for your time and assistance in advance!

Sincerely,

Robert Singh, Research Assistant
UIC Institute for Entrepreneurial Studies

Enclosures

WORDING USED FOR POSTCARD REMINDER:

JUST A REMINDER

Several weeks ago, you should have received a copy of a mail survey questionnaire. If you have already filled out the questionnaire and returned it to the UIC Institute for Entrepreneurial Studies, please disregard this reminder. If you have not yet filled out your questionnaire, your generous donation of 15 minutes would be greatly appreciated! You will receive a management summary for your use.

If you did not receive a copy of the questionnaire or you need another copy, please call Rob Singh at (312) 996-6372 or send an email to "rsingh2@uic.edu". Thank you!

We hope you and yours have a wonderful holiday season!

Index